# Communication
## A Circumspection



Bhanuvikraman Nair

ATLANTIC
PUBLISHERS & DISTRIBUTORS (P) LTD

Published by
**ATLANTIC**
PUBLISHERS & DISTRIBUTORS (P) LTD
7/22, Ansari Road, Darya Ganj,
New Delhi-110002
Phones : +91-11-40775252, 23273880, 23275880, 23280451
Fax : +91-11-23285873
Web : www.atlanticbooks.com
E-mail : orders@atlanticbooks.com

Branch Office
5, Nallathambi Street, Wallajah Road,
Chennai-600002
Phones : +91-44-64611085, 32413319
E-mail : chennai@atlanticbooks.com



ISBN 978-81-269-1555-2



Printed in India at Nice Printing Press, A-33/3A, Site-IV, Industrial Area, Sahibabad, Ghaziabad, U.P.

***Dedicated to***

The everlasting memory of
My beloved parents

# Acknowledgements

I am indebted to all beings of this beautiful globe, members of fauna and even flora, who have been my best teachers. Whatever bit of empirical knowledge that I could gather has mainly come about as a by-product of my childlike keen observations on their individualistic as well as collective behaviour at various stages and situations, and so also my interactions with them. The output of these observations and interactions has then been brought to micro-focus and analysed, to the extent of my capability, with proportionate tinge of real and imaginative projections on them.

I hereby express my special gratitude to Dr. Gopakumar G Nair, former President of Indian Drugs Manufacturers' Association, for writing Foreword to this book. Dr. Kumar has had over forty years of experience in the industrial world where he has held positions of Director, Chairman & Managing Director of a reputed Pharmaceutical Enterprise in Mumbai.

I wish to express my gratitude to all those respected and devoted English teachers, who taught me various aspects of English language and literature. I hold all of them in my esteemed memory, especially late Prof. C.A. Sheppard. I also thank my eldest brother Lt. Col. N.P. Nair (Retd.) who had trained me in communication in English.

Last but not least, I thank Atlantic Publishers & Distributors (P) Ltd., for the interest evinced in publishing this book.

**Bhanuvikraman Nair**

# Foreword

Communication is integral to bonding in today's fast-paced world more than ever before. Its importance needs no stressing. Communicative interactions exist between and among members of the fauna and flora, and various elements of the Great Nature. Interactions also exist between and among the Sun, Planets and their Moons in our Solar System. We have every right to imagine and conceive that there could be a communicative link-up between and among the millions of Solar Systems of the Universe. Believe it or not, some "chosen souls" amongst us have access to a 'hotline' system of communication directly with God Almighty—we call it 'communion'. In a nutshell, we can say that communication is all-pervasive and ever relevant.

Man is a social animal. Most of the members of the fauna too exist in societies. A society stands for group activities. A group may be homogeneous or heterogeneous. Exchange of thoughts—communication—is the thread that binds individual members together in a society and hence it forms the quintessential part of any social living. It is vital for the very sustenance of any society. In fact, a definition of the word 'society' will connote and include communication. Man is a thinking animal. His thoughts encompass all aspects of the art of his living. Thoughts are communicated and dessiminated for the use of all the members of man's society.

I feel greatly privileged, proud and extremely happy to write a few words in the form of a Foreword to this book entitled, *Communication: A Circumspection*, written by my good old friend, Bhanuvikraman Nair. I have read his previous work, *Random Reflections*, and have been greatly impressed by the way he has expressed flippantly and frankly his views on many of the human traits prominently exhibited by humans themselves in intra-social interactions. In the present book, *Communication: A Circumspection*, he has briefly communicated, in particular to the students of Management, the most quintessential aspect of societal living, i.e. communicating. Inclusion as well as essaying of topics like, Soliloquy, Silence, Braggartism and Telepathy in the realm of communication, are quite interesting and as such the most striking features of this work. His fairly long experience as a Senior Officer of the Indian Air Force has encouraged him to muse about communicative system being followed in the Military Organizations. I must say that the last two topics, "A Canine Perspective" and "A Speaking Bed", appearing in Part IV of the book, with their thought-provoking potential, would instil implosion of interest in the minds of his enlightened readers. As a whole, the book can very well be thought of as a wholesome mini-compendium of information on communication. I am sure that the book shall be of great help to one-and-all, especially to fresher-students of Management. I sincerely wish the book and its author all the best.

**Dr. Gopakumar G Nair**
Former President,
Indian Drug Manufacturers' Association

# Contents

# Introduction

Right from birth, all organisms start communicating. A newborn baby cries as soon as it comes out of the womb. This is probably its first piece of communication. It conveys to Nature that it needs oxygen to breathe and the Nature provides it. The infant again cries expressing its need for food and its understanding mother meets its requirements. "Milk is given only to a crying child" is a famous adage. In each of these cases a two-way communication is complete even without a word being uttered. This system of communication continues between the infant and the mother till the former develops a medium, efficient enough to meet its requirements for survival. It learns a language instinctively from its mother. The mother trains and conditions the child.

The history of evolution and development of communication is the same as that of human civilization. The advent and existence of both of these have been more accidental than designed by anyone; they have been developed through gradual natural organic processes slowly and steadily over many a millennium. Thus they are self-created and developed, and communication did design, foster, transform culture and perpetuate societies. This system, by and large, has been followed in case of the entire fauna kingdom as well.

Humans were physically not as strong as many others in the jungle. Individually, humans had to face many problems which even threatened their survival. It was this survival instinct that had brought them together. Initially, they had felt the need to protect their young ones from other wild animals—a common animal attribute. Living as a family was the first step towards formation of societies. Humans had instinctively understood that union is strength. Gradually they started grouping of families. Thus, Societies were born. Similarly, all other members of the fauna too started living together as groups or some sort of societies. These were all part of grand natural organic evolution gradually taking place in the living world. Most important catalytic element in it had been communication. Their communicative skills developed, and with that their mental horizon became widened. All this happened slowly and gradually, consuming many a millennium.

Man is a thinking animal. This trait in him distinguishes him from many other living organisms. His thoughts encompass all aspects of the art of his living. He is not living alone in this world. His thoughts, howsoever lofty, will have no utility in the context of societal living if he chooses to keep them preserved in his mind alone. When he leaves the world on cessation of his earthly innings, these thoughts would also be buried in his coffin along with him. On the other hand, if he leaves them behind, it would be of great help in terms of enhancing the quality of life of others, still left behind by him, to live in the world. So he has to communicate and disseminate his thoughts. This is how we can conceive of continuity of life. 'Life' carries on in the same way as a baton of athletic 'relay race', getting transferred from the hand of the first participant to that of the second of the group and so on. And the relay race carries on. The baton does not disappear unlike the participants. People come and go but their thoughts are forever. These thoughts and actions become traditions for the successive generations and these traditions subsequently are sunk into culture and civilization. It is a slow and gradual organic transformation. The origin of this kind of process is prehistoric. Group activities are the essence of societal living. In this it is imperative that information and knowledge acquired by one and all are shared among all the members of the society through interactional transactions and webs of communication. But for this, our societies would not have flourished and attained advancement as we witness today. Communication plays its quintessential role.

Communication in many of its facets is not limited to humans, or even to primates. Every information exchange—transmission and reception of signals—between or among all living organisms can be considered as a part of the whole web of communication. Animal communication is any behaviour on the part of one animal that has an effect on the current or future behaviour of another animal. Of course, human communication can be subsumed as a highly developed form of animal communication. The study of animal communication has played an important part in the development of ethnology, sociobiology, and the study of animal cognition. Although animals communicate, they do not have language like what the humans have. They do make noises but these tend to be situation-related—for example, a loud shriek to signify fear or severe pain. Even humans have situation-related noises. An Indian, an Englishman and a Russian, standing blind-folded would make the same noise if someone stamped on their toes. All of them smile or laugh in the same manner when they are happy with some pleasing thing or situation. All human infants in the world cry in the same manner when they encounter unpleasant or irritable situations. Facial expressions at the sight of terrifying object—for example, sight of an attacking lion—would be of the same type in all cases. These are examples of the ways of communication.

Understanding of the animal world in general is a rapidly growing field. We have witnessed in the current century so far, that many prior understandings related to diverse fields such as their emotions, culture and learning, and even sexual conduct, long thought to be well understood, have been revolutionized. Humans are able to communicate with animals employed in circuses. However, these animals have to learn a special modified means of communication. Animals can learn human language to some extent as understood recently with respect to dolphin communication and teaching hand signals to apes. Some dogs are taught by humans to sing songs sung by them. It is a pity that the humans with great level of intelligence are unable to learn the language of the less 'intelligent' animals. Instead they have to force them to learn theirs!

Communication is a process. Oxygen and water are the two most important elements required for the very existence of all living organisms, but none is conscious about their importance except in their absence or inadequacy of supply. Similar is the case with communication. Communication comes to the rescue of a breathless patient asking for remedying breathlessness or a thirsty person for a glass of water. Communication forms, thus, an important ingredient required for the very survival of living beings. Communication takes place automatically without the consent or request of anyone. It is a process which most of us never think about analytically. Any breakdown of it culminates in all kinds of maladies. People, who analyse the use and the usefulness of this process, gain immensely in terms of an unusual insight into human nature. If people were unable to share knowledge, each person would have to learn everything himself. There are various ways through which living beings communicate with one another. They manage it by tongue, teeth, mouth, nose, eyes, face, head, shoulders, hands, legs, i.e. whole body, through singing, laughing, dancing, weeping, touching and even by silence. In short, they use all the resources at their command for the purpose of communication. They share their ideas and emotions, actions and reactions through this communication with other members of their societies.

The subject matter of the book *Communication: A Circumspection* has been divided into four parts. Part I deals with human communication in general—a circumspection. Besides general aspects of communication, soliloquy and silence, both of which represent some element or semblance of communication, have been discussed. Some special features that we observe in the system of communication being practiced in armed forces are highlighted briefly in the essay entitled 'Communication in Military Context'.

Contained in Part II, are essays on 'Telepathic Communication', 'Role of Humour in Communication' and 'Counselling'. 'Braggartism' and 'Sarcasm, Derision and Insultation' are special or peculiar types of communication taking place amongst human beings.

Contained in Part III, are communication vis-à-vis other members of the fauna and that with respect to flora.

In Part IV, there are two narrations: the first, dealing with the saga of existence of a personified inanimate object, bed, in 'A Speaking Bed' and the second, a candid self-analytical account of the life of a pet-dog in 'A Canine Perspective'. Both these narrations are in autobiographical mode.

The book shall be useful to students and teachers of communication, especially the details that are related to evolution and techniques of communication. It shall be equally useful for people involved in management studies, counselling, and other fields where communication is the key. Common readers shall also find it interesting and informative.

**Bhanuvikraman Nair**

# PART I

# 1

# Communication: A Circumspection

Man is a thinking animal. This trait in him makes him different from many other living organisms. His thoughts encompass all aspects of the art of his living. He is not living alone in this world. His thoughts, howsoever lofty, will have no utility in the context of societal living if he chooses to keep them preserved in his mind alone. When he leaves the world on cessation of his earthly innings, these thoughts would also be buried along with him. On the other hand, if he leaves them behind, it would be of great help for others still left living in the world. So he has to communicate and disseminate his thoughts, thereby enhancing the quality of life of his fellow beings left behind. Group activities are the essence of societal living. In this it is imperative that information and knowledge acquired by him are shared among all the members of his society by interactional transactions. But for this, our societies would not have flourished and attained advancement as we witness today. This all is the result of communication.

Communication is sharing information or providing entertainment. Probably, the most important type of communication is personal communication which happens when people make their thoughts and wishes known to one another. Without personal communication, parents would not know what their children want; teachers could not help their students learn; friends could not make plans with one another. In fact, human beings could not have survived as a society so long but for communication. Another type of communication happens when messages are sent to large audience: we call it mass communication. The media for this are books, television, newspapers, radio and the like.

## Development of Communication

In pre-historic times long before they developed actual words, people probably communicated with one another by sound and gestures. We can guess that language must have begun as an imitation of sounds in Nature, such as howling of wind, sound from waterfalls, sonant notes emanating from friction among clustered trees, bird-songs, splash murmurs of rivers, barking, growling, howling and roaring of animals and the like. After the advent of language, people exchanged views and news chiefly by word of mouth. Runners carried spoken messages over long distances. People also used drum-beats, fires and smoke signals to communicate with other people who could understand those codes used. Paintings and drawings were the first step towards a written language. Pre-historic artists began to use a series of pictures to tell a story, such as the history of a good hunting trip or violent storm. Gradually, they developed small pictures that stood for most common objects and ideas—the hieroglyphic or pictographic writing. For all these developments, it took millions of years; it has been a very slow evolution. It is surprising to see that only in the last few centuries of human civilisation human beings could make notable strides in its development. It would be sheer childishness, impiety and even blasphemy on our part to ask or even think as to what our ancestors had been doing till then. After a couple of centuries hence, if we, the present generation, survive, to state optimistically, our successors would include us too in the ancestral fold and might hold us responsible for not making notable strides, considering the present unimaginable galloping trend of development in the field of communication. Oh, Lord, pardon them then! It has been a natural organic evolution. It needs to understand that the evolution and development of communication have been a great impetus for the development of our brains as well, and that is how we are able to think now like that. After that, the process of development got accelerated. The sequence of evolution and development in brief is as follows:

Paintings and drawings, hieroglyphic system of writing and communicating, invention of paper, invention of pencil of graphite, printing machine, photography, electric telegraphy, typewriter, telephones, wireless telegraphy, radio, television, xerox, teleprinter, satellite communication, mobile phones, laser, fibre optics and God knows what more to follow!

Communication is the process of disseminating information from a sender to a receiver with the use of a medium. Communication requires that all parties have an area of communicative commonality and mutual relevance. It is defined as a process by which we assign and convey meaning, in an attempt to create shared understanding. This process requires an inexhaustible inventory of skills in intrapersonal and interpersonal processing, listening, observing, speaking, questioning, analyzing and evaluating. Use of this process is developmental, and transfers to all areas of life: home, school, community, work, and beyond. It is through communication that collaboration and co-operation are elicited.

**Dynamics of Communication:**

| Sender | Conceiving | Message |
|---|---|---|
| | Encoding | Message |
| | Selecting | Medium |
| Receiver | Decoding | Message |
| | Interpreting | Message |
| | Feedback | (Response) |
| Sender | Receiving | Feedback |
| | Evaluating | Effect |
| | Satisfied | Not satisfied |
| | Thinking | Further course |

The sender takes the decision to send a message, as a result of some impulse, thought process or some external stimulus. Then he chooses an appropriate language or combination of written, spoken or non-verbal communication most suitable for the type of communication. He makes sure, by carefully avoiding ambiguity and vagueness, so that the message is not misinterpreted and misunderstood. After logical structuring of the idea, he chooses very apt words, gestures or any other ways as vehicles keeping the overall context in mind. He is careful in assessing the emotional state of the receiver. It is always better to empathise the receiver's position. When composing a message, the sender must decide what action or response he wants from the recipient of the message. Thereafter he selects an appropriate medium which is most likely to achieve his aim. Some of the messages make no use of language at all, they are the non-verbal communication. The road signs, for example, form universal non-verbal communication and are understood by all nationalities alike.

### Media

The media may be written, oral and visual. The best communication is two-way, longitudinally downward and upward and laterally. The principal medium is the written one. It consists of letters, memos, minutes, notes, telex, advertisements and press release. It provides written record and proof of dispatch and receipt. It can comfortably relay complex ideas, and provide analysis, evaluation and summary. It can be duplicated. It can confirm, interpret and clarify oral communication. It has some disadvantages too. It takes time and can be expensive and more formal. It can cause problems of interpretation. There is no possibility of instant feedback. Messages can not be modified once made out and sent. Exchanges of views and attitudes are possible only over a period of time.

The second medium of communication is oral. It consists of face-to-face conversations, talks, speeches, conferences, telephones, intercom, video, interviews and meetings. This direct medium ensures physical proximity, instant interchange of opinions and instant feedback. Through this medium, it is easier to convince and persuade those who receive the messages. It also ensures participation of all concerned and their direct contributions. It offers some disadvantages too. It is very difficult to hold ground in face of opposition. It is rather difficult to control the proceedings if the number of people attending is more; often disputes and discords might arise. Moreover, the quality of decision-making may be inferior.

The third option is visual communication. It is non-verbal. It consists of visual aids and other reinforcing tools such as dictating machines, tape recorders, graphs, OHP, posters, film slides, charts, voice, face and body language. These visual aids reinforce oral communication by adding visual stimulus. It seeks to simplify efforts in written and oral media. A melodious song sung by an expert musician *per se* can enthrall an audience. But if an Indian classical dancer performs narrating the meaning of that song through his or her dance symbols using various expressions by the eyes, fingers, hands, feet and the whole of body, the song can produce maximum effect on the audience. The attire that the dancer wears and the scene settings matching to the soul of that song will enhance the effect to greater heights. All these form visual aids that reinforce and supplement various elements in the oral communication. The visual aids quantify ideas in number form as well. Also situations can be simulated. Conversely, should there be any difficulty in interpretation of data offered in the visuals one can employ written or spoken words to supplement them. It calls for additional skills for comprehension and interpretation. It is quite an expensive medium.

Communication is the means of sending a message through different media whether it be verbal or non-verbal, so long as a being transmits a thought-provoking idea, gesture, action, and the like. Communication is a learned skill. Most people are born with the physical ability to talk, but we must learn to speak well and communicate effectively. Speaking, listening, and our ability to understand verbal and non-verbal meanings are skills we develop in various ways. We learn basic communication skills by observing other people and modelling our behaviours based on what we see. We also are taught some communication skills directly through education, and by practising those skills and having them evaluated, we become better equipped communicators.

Communication as an academic discipline that relates to all the ways we communicate, so it embraces a large body of study and knowledge. The communication discipline includes both verbal and non-verbal messages. A body of scholarship all about communication is presented and explained in textbooks, electronic publications, and academic journals. In the journals, researchers report the results of studies that are the bases for an ever expanding understanding of how we all communicate. Communication happens at many levels; even for one single action, there will be many different ways. Several, if not all, fields of study dedicate a portion of attention to communication. So when speaking about communication it is very important to be sure about what aspects of communication one is speaking about. Definitions of communication range widely, some recognizing that animals can communicate with each other as well as human beings, and some are more narrow, only including human beings within the parameters of human symbolic interactions.

## Communication among Children

Children are bestowed with abundant capacity of curiosity. They are highly curious about the world and its multifarious manifestations. It is the duty of teachers and elders to help them explore ways to use this faculty in positive ways that will render them self-motivated and independent learners. For this, learning to communicate is very important. Young children have a natural investigative style of learning and an equally natural urge to communicate their discoveries. By communicating their ideas, children are able to demonstrate their curiosity and express their creativity. The science and technology aspects of knowledge and understanding of the world as they perceive provide an ideal opportunity to help them develop communication skills. They start developing their own ideas about their world and how it works. Although our image of science may be about 'doing' things, in fact it is far more about communicating theories, both to ourselves and to others. The process of science involves observing, raising questions, hypothsising, predicting, planning and carrying out investigation, interpreting results and sharing findings. A wide range of oral communication skills can be developed through scientific exploration. Children will have opportunities to experiment with language and practise the skills of explaining, questioning, hypothesising and predicting. They will be keen to find ways to influence others and persuade them to accept the 'correctness' of their findings. All scientists need the acknowledgement of others that what they have discovered is 'true for the time being'. Scientific discovery, from the Nobel Prize winner to the toddler investigating jelly, needs to be shared with others in order to be validated.

It is often a co-operative activity involving more than one child, such as a design technology project, that can help children to see how individual decisions contribute to a larger group project. They will begin to appreciate the value of clear and accurate explanations, and learn to appreciate feedback from their group. There will be many opportunities to use 'specialist' vocabulary and communicate through oral, graphic and mathematical representations. Scientific and technological ideas can be communicated through speaking, drawing, writing, constructing, music and dance, each of which will be of value in different situations. In every group of children there will be 'experts'—children who are fascinated by machines, by construction, by the planets, by plants and animals—with knowledge, skills and experience to communicate. Creating opportunities for ideas to be shared will help children to develop the skills to communicate scientific ideas effectively. This will help them to learn how to express their ideas clearly, take turns in discussion, listen to the points of view of others and negotiate. Explorations and investigations provide many opportunities for using mark-making and writing skills. Capitalise on these by creating reasons to produce labels, to sequence events and to write instructions. Drawings and pictures convey meaning and can be used to initiate, develop and communicate ideas. Children who find difficulty in using language may prefer to express their ideas through drawings, but all children will benefit from the challenge of trying to convey their thinking through graphic representation using pictures, plans, maps and diagrams. When a child re-presents his ideas and thoughts in a drawing he is also re-presenting them to himself. In doing this he modifies his ideas and develops his reasoning skills. By then, going on to explain his drawings to a group, he has a further opportunity to revisit, revise and enrich his understanding. We should remember to recognise and value the very wide range of languages which young children use to communicate. Some children may prefer to express their design ideas and scientific theories using the language of the body as well as the brain. They will communicate their ideas and thinking through models, construction, music, dance and re-enactment.

Communication is usually described along a few major dimensions: content (what type of things are communicated), source, emmisor, sender or encoder (by whom), form (in which form), channel (through which medium), destination, receiver, target or decoder (to whom), and the purpose of the pragmatic aspect. Between parties, communication includes acts that confer knowledge and experiences, give advice and commands, and ask questions. These acts may take many forms, in one of the various manners of communication. The form depends on the abilities of the group communicating. Together, communication content and form make messages that are sent towards a destination. The target can be oneself, another person or being, another entity (such as a corporation or group of beings).

## Barriers of Communication

Many people think that communicating is easy. It is after all something we have done all our lives. There is some truth in this simplistic view. Communicating is straightforward. What makes it complex, difficult, and frustrating are the barriers we put in the way. There are a few barriers or impediments in communication. They relate to physical non-proximity of those who communicate, individual perceptual problems, emotional dimensions, cultural ethos, language used, gender consciousness and mental blocks in interpersonal approaches.

Each workplace is to be seen as a social set-up. All the workers, irrespective of their position or status should be able to interact freely. They should not be separated by doors, screens or walls. One of the most important factors in building cohesive teams and *esprit de corps* is proximity. As long as people still have a personal space that they can call their own; nearness to others aids communication because it helps them get to know one another. Their "Hellow"s and "How are you"s when they meet first time at the commencement of their working schedules mean a lot. Each individual sees the world differently and hence the need of communication. This is what we call individual perception and it cohabits with all individuals at all times. None can evade it, and it has its influence every time people try to communicate. One of the chief barriers to free and open communications is related to emotional dimensions. It comprises mainly of fear, mistrust and suspicion. "Harry-don't" attitude of parents, teachers and elders while dealing with their wards would nip any tendency of the children in the bud to be free and frank in their approaches to others and their very on going life itself.

Culture interferes with effective cross-cultural understanding. People form perceptions of the world and make them terms of reference. Culture groups offer special spectacles to each of their members on subsidised rates or even free of cost. These members through these spectacles try to view any new input of information. They develop and conceive notions that they like to hold dearly. These pre-conceived beliefs and notions cause probable loss of sight of actual characteristics of the new information. Culture sets rules or norms for patterns of behaviour of people, and because of this people belonging to different cultures behave differently. Even display of emotions by people belonging to different cultures is too quite wide and varied. Effective communication with people of different cultures is especially challenging. Cultures provide people with ways of thinking, ways of seeing, hearing, and interpreting the world. They have a role in the formation of the cognitive system of individuals. Cultures determine behavioural parameters as well as ways of expression of emotions. There are marked differences in patterns of working of cultures on the individuals who subscribe to them; these cultural ethos influence communication outputs. If the people involved are not aware of the potential for such problems, they are even more likely to fall victims to them, although it takes more than awareness to overcome these problems, and to communicate effectively across cultures. The same words can mean different things to people from different cultures, even when they have a common language.

When the languages are different, and translation has to be resorted to communicate, the potential for misunderstandings increases. Language that describes what we want to say in our terms may present barriers to others who are not familiar with our ways of expressions. When we use such 'unfamiliar' language as well as expressions, it may mean a way of excluding others. In a global context the greatest compliment we can pay to others is to talk in their language.

Other factors affecting or influencing communication include situation context, degree of formality or informality and non-verbal clues like facial expressions, gestures by hands, arms, shoulders, eyes, head, and general body language. The ability to communicate is special but it is often taken for granted and it is not always used to the greatest advantage. There are a few factors. Messages could wrongly be conceived, making them vague and ambiguous. This is affected by the existing relationships between the sender and the receiver. Also message might have been encoded in wrong language or inappropriate tone. It could be because of a wrong choice of medium due to which offence might have been caused, wasting time and incurring wasteful expenses. On the other side, communication is affected if either feedback is not given due to any valid reason or the received feedback is misinterpreted by the sender and misunderstood by the receiver.

No matter how good and effective a communicator one may be, yet the fact is that one does face certain barriers, from time to time, which force them to work on becoming even more effective in their skills to communicate, while listening, speaking and in the case of employment of non-verbal communications. Let us analyse some of them.

### *Listening Barriers*

(a) Interrupting the speaker.

(b) Not maintaining eye-contact with the speaker.

(c) Rushing the speaker to complete what he/she has to say.

(d) Making the speaker feel as though he/she is wasting the listener's time.

(e) Being distracted by something that is not part of the on-going communication.

(f) Getting ahead of the speaker and completing his/her thoughts.

(g) Ignoring the speaker's requests.

(h) Topping the speaker's story with one's own set of examples.

(i) Forgetting what is being discussed.

(j) Asking too many questions, for the sake of probing.

### *Barriers While Speaking*

(a) Lack of clarity in messages.

(b) Lack of consistency in the communication process.

(c) Incomplete sentences.

(d) Not understanding the receiver.

(e) Not seeking clarifications while communicating.

### *The Other Barriers*

(a) An individual's subjective viewpoint towards issues/people, which leads to assumptions.

(b) An emotional block, which can lead to an attitude of indifference, suspicion or hostility toward the subject.

(c) An emotional block or bias that is based on a third party's points of view, or on what one has read/heard.

(d) Words can have different meanings to different people, thus blocking communication.

(e) Use of negative words.

One should do a self-analysis and self-appraisal of one's performance every time immediately after completing his part of communication. He should understand that the most important barrier in communication is not of listening; the main problem lies with the communicator himself. The following points are worth considering:

(1) One should unbiasedly check if one's expectations from the listener have correctly been conveyed to the listener and the latter understands them as such. There should not be any gap. This often does not happen.

(2) One should have self-confidence and get rid of any possible anxiety or fear of rejection of his ideas by the other side.

(3) One should avoid use of words such as 'never', 'always', 'forever'. They often make a statement untrue. Use a less absolute word. It becomes unbelievable when someone says, "I saw it with my own eyes" or "I swear I saw or heard it".

(4) Do not hurt anyone, for this may make him feel foolish or stupid, and consequently he may exclude himself from further participation.

The following anecdote is a reminder of how our thoughts, assumptions and perceptions shape our own realities:

A traveller was walking down a road when he met a man from the next town. "Excuse me", he said. "I am hoping to stay in the next town tonight. Can you tell me what the townspeople are like?" "Well," said the townsman, "How did you find the people in the last town you visited?" "Oh, they were an unsociable bunch. Kept to themselves. Took me for a fool. Over-charged me for what I got. Gave me very poor service." "Well, then," said the townsman, "You'll find them pretty much the same here".

## Effective Communication

We have seen that there are many barriers, hindrances or impediments in our efforts to have a sound and foolproof communication system. In order, therefore, to achieve effective communication, we have to address the various barriers and remove them.

Any piece of communication is considered effective if it serves its intended purpose efficiently, effectively and economically. The criteria in a nutshell are:

(a) The message received by the receiver is the same or very close to what is sent. Any breach of continuity results in misrepresentation leading to misunderstanding which could often be dangerous in the ultimate analysis.

(b) The verbal and the non-verbal elements in it are not to be in conflict with each other. They should be compatible and congruent. A good system of back-up by an instant feedback can ensure this compatibility.

(c) The designed response of the message is evoked. The sender should be able to influence and motivate the receiver to act according to the designs envisaged in the message.

(d) Ultimately the communication must serve to building-up an ideal relationship between the sender and the receiver. Harmony is the key word.

(e) If, while encoding the message, the sender exercises economy of effort in terms of time and symbols without jeopardizing clarity and overtness, the receiver will get it right.

All of us are bestowed with communication skills. Expert communicators can use their skills effectively as we can witness with politicians and television presenters. Communication is also subject to abuse. A look at wartime propaganda shows how information can be transmitted in certain ways to achieve a particular effect. A comparison of newspaper articles covering the same news items will often reveal that some facts are being selected and interpreted for a particular purpose—

perhaps to protect the ruling political power, to sensationalize scandalous aspects or to manipulate public opinion to a particular way of thinking by selecting and articulating mischievous words and adopting apparently convincing ways of presentation. Analysis of newspaper reports prior to general elections is particularly fruitful in this respect.

# 2

# Communication in Business Organizations

We, as social beings, cannot carry on with our day-to-day lives without communicating between and among the members of our society. This is more so in business activities. Business needs people who can communicate because communication is essential for business operations. Business rewards good communicators. The flow of communication in a business organization forms a complex and ever-changing network. Good communication is necessary in any job, but especially in positions that involve interaction with clients and company management. One must be able to convey information and ideas to these people clearly, concisely and eloquently, if not, the spirit of the messages will get lost. This includes all forms of communication; verbal, written and even body language. The initial impression one makes on people will be determined by how well he or she communicates with others. "The first impression is the best." It serves to build up trust and teamwork among employees. Communication has a direct bearing on productivity; if it is clear to people as to what actually is expected of them, they would work more efficiently.

Managers are leaders. They manage the affairs of their organizations by leading the men working under them. This is not possible without a proper system of communication working between the manager and the other employees. Developing excellent communication skills and employing them effectively and efficiently to the best advantage of the organization is what is expected of a manager. He must be able to share information, ideas and knowledge in order to instil enthusiasm and motivation among his men. For that, he has to communicate clearly with each member of his group. It is not enough if a manager gives out information, ideas or orders to his subordinates; he should be willing to listen and receive ideas from them, whether he likes them or not. Communication is complete only if it is made two-way, that is, downward and upward.

Communication can be:

(a) Formal Internal

(b) Informal Internal

(c) Formal External

Formal internal can be downward, upward or lateral. Downward communication relates to passing orders and instructions from the top order of hierarchic echelons to the lower ones on matters concerning the goals, objectives, mission and policies and methods of achieving them and so also instructions and orders concerning the day-to-day operation of the organization. This communication originates from the President or CEO of the organization and its essence and spirit permeate vertically as well as laterally downwards to the bottom layers following the formal lines of organization. The system followed is like the network of arteries and veins in the body system. Business has well-established channels of information flow. They are required to be followed by all. Usually they take the form of letters, office memos, minutes of conferences and meetings and other forms of written communications.

There takes place oral communication too, such as face-to-face briefing, telephonic and intercom conversations, meetings and conferences in order to interpret, complement or supplement general orders for facilitating day-to-day working of various units, departments and sections of the organization.

There is the formal upward communication, that is, from the lower hierarchic echelons to the higher ones. It can take place from workers to their foremen, from foremen to their supervising managers and so on, up to the level of CEO and the organizational President. Usually there are reports on compliance with the orders or instructions, and achievements, shortfalls, shortcomings, suggestions and many other matters. The periodicity of such reports will be determined by the criterion of importance and situational characteristics. The periodicity may range from hourly to yearly or even longer periods of time. These reports serve to form bases for evaluating performance of the various departments as well as personnel at various levels. Some of them might even influence future decision-making. These reports are generally written communications; some of them may be rendered on telephones or intercoms or through e-mails, depending on the nature of information or situational demands of time-element.

Parallel to the formal network, there runs a secondary network of informal or personal communication. It comprises of thousands of pieces of personal communications occurring in business, characterized by their ever-changing and complex structure. It links all members of the organization and follows no set pattern, a haphazard and non-uniform entity. Individuals form several social groups on and off the floor and interact. These social transactions result in large volumes of information, related or unrelated to their working environment. The larger the organization, the more groups and sub-groups will be formed, and thereby more nodal points in the informal communication network will be formed leading to more complexities. This network is known as 'grapevine'. This is a mill whose outputs are gossip and rumour. This is far more effective and fast a communication system than the formal one. It can determine the course of the organization itself. Some managers to their detriment do not recognize its existence. Only a transparent and just demeanour and dealing on the part of the management can create a harmless and productive grapevine. It can be profitably and effectively made use of by clever managers for circulating healthy but tricky information. They convert such information into a rumour-look-like, through concealment and camouflaging and feed into the grapevine network; the information would reach all much faster than through official or formal channels. One has to remember always the caution, "Handle with care".

External communication is the one that a business does with people and groups outside the business like suppliers, service providers, customers and the general public. It also includes all efforts at direct selling, printing brochures, advertising (print, audio and video media), point-o-purchase display aids, efforts for ideal public relations and image building, etcetera.

Formal external communication means all about business. We may adopt any media for this purpose. The first impact one person makes on others is often through words on paper, the written medium. This means that in many instances the first and the only opportunity one has to influence others is by one's skill at putting one's thought on paper. The most common forms of written that one is likely to come across in business are the letters. A written communication is more accurate, permanent and suitable mode than telephonic one. There are some principles that are required to be kept in mind. These principles are concerned with purpose, content, structure, style and layout. The purpose may be to inform and to influence the recipient. The information may be new to the recipient, or a confirmation to an already given information; and in either case, the language used has to be polite as well as brief. "Smoking in public places is prohibited. The offenders will be severely dealt with", an official administrative notification says. Here it sounds that the authorities are sure, to begin with, that this order would not be complied with. The warning element in the notification is rude, crude and superfluous and it carries a negative and upsetting impact. It could have been avoided.

The brevity should not be at the cost of clarity and precision. In order to influence someone, one has to convince him that he had specifically kept him in his mind when he was writing the letter. The contents depend on the subject matter. The letter should be structured carefully. It should have a beginning, middle and end. The first paragraph should state about the reason for the letter in brief and succinct, and in a manner that can infuse interest in the reader. The middle should elucidate the contents of the first. The ending should clearly express what action the writer hopes or expects of the recipient to take. Above all, the vocabulary chosen must match as closely as the writer can think of what the level of knowledge and education of the recipient. A printed letter-head is usually used, but the layout can be suitably modified to suit to the overall requirement. Keeping all these points in mind, the writer endeavours to make out a draft which after proper scrutiny can be changed into the 'fair' one.

The following points should be kept in mind while making out a communication in writing:

(a) As far as the style is concerned, one should prefer short, concrete and active words to long, abstract, passive ones.

(b) Each line of thought should be dealt with in new paragraphs.

(c) Avoidance of words with negative meanings and connotations and unpleasantness, as far as possible.

(d) Emphasis on 'You-view' rather than 'I-view'.

(e) Avoidance of tendency to be formal.

(f) Single-out the reader. One should adapt to his reader. For that, that one has to select words and sentences that the reader understands. One should use words that are simple, familiar and short and with precise meanings, but the selected words with adequate strength, deserving emphasis and vigour. Words should be used economically. Use words that the reader understands and sentences so structured as to help the reader to organize the message in his mind clearly; writing should be adapted and addressed directly to the reader. All readers do not have high reading ability. The message should be brief but not at the cost of clarity and effectiveness. It is always better to write messages in conversational style. Avoid discriminatory ones, against women, nationality, age or disability.

(g) Avoidance of show of anger.

(h) Avoidance of overdose of goodwill exercise.

(i) Carefulness in not to be or appear to be insincere.

(j) When a bad news is to be conveyed, it is imperative that the message should begin with buffer. It should be conveyed diplomatically, unless sure of its being received in routine manner. A convincing explanation reflecting positive attitude will be ideal in cases of refusals or denials. Always end the message with a positive note.

The introduction of the word processor to the office environment has revolutionized communication system. The necessity to store large quantities of paper documents in cumbersome and space-consuming filing cabinets has been considerably reduced. It is now possible to retain vast quantities of information on a hard disk incorporated into the computer, or on a number of floppy disks. The process of exchange of information via a word processor is relatively simple, besides being ultimately very cheap and economical. Data such as letters, reports, circulars, memoranda are inserted into formatted floppy disks, and at any time, required number of hard copies or prints-out can be obtained from them easily at will. Text can be altered with ease. There are many facilities available such as changing of the order of paragraphs, sentences or words, checking and correcting of spellings and grammar, providing different print emphases, possibilities of producing personalized letters for circulation to desired number of clients. Filing is simplified as all information is stored on disks, and security or back-up copies are too kept. It should, however, be understood that confidentiality of information can not be kept in word processing system. The word processors facilitate both the distribution and exchange of information and have had a dramatic impact on the business world.

Today, electronic mail, e-mail in short, is a common mainstream form of business communication. The rapid growth of e-mail has been the most exciting development in business communication in recent years. Postal services have been rendered redundant. E-mail communication is widely used in all types and sizes of organizations. It has clear advantages over its main competitor, the telephones. The e-mail is the most widely used form of written communication in business. Although heavily used for communicating with outside parties, it is a well-utilized means for internal written communication between and among people in the organization for formal as well as informal purposes. Some formal reports to higher-ups are sent by e-mails.

The main advantages are as follows:

(a) It is expeditious; it leads to fast decisions.

(b) It involves personal touch.

(c) The cost incurred will be minimal.

(d) There is no need for synchronizing time, thereby ensuring that there are no interruptions in the mental work of anyone.

(e) The mail processing can be done leisurely at one's own pace, according to earmarked priorities; hence time-management is taken care of.

(f) Transfer of emotions is avoided, and a matter-of-fact approach can be adopted.

(g) People find it easier to tell the truth via e-mail. Difficult pieces can be mulled over and shaped in the least painful manner without affecting the core message. It is easier to refuse at times which is difficult in a face-to-face communication. It is easier to withstand a mental pressure imposed by others. It is easier to minimize the hurt to the other person's feelings while being unmoved in one's stand.

(h) Multiple contacts are possible. Due to savings in time per contact and improved memory system, many more contacts can be handled easily than in a conversation mode.

(i) All messages can be searched and recovered in seconds.

There are, however, some disadvantages too. They are mainly as follows:

(a) There is lack of confidentiality in information.

(b) Emotions of the individuals involved are not conveyed.

(c) There can be delays in treatment and disposal of mail received due to volume.

(d) There is no instant feedback.

(e) Some activities like brainstorming session or interviews can not be done.

(f) Many people will take offence if you tell them you prefer to talk to them via e-mail.

(g) Fun of direct communication is lost. Adding fun to communication may not be cost effective, but its value can be immense for health, sociability and human contact.

(h) Without necessary skills, benefits of e-mail are often lost. Some people simply do not like e-mail, and they may be lost to the cause of e-mail brainstorming.

**Report Writing**

A business report is an orderly and objective communication of factual information that serves a business purpose. Hence reports are prepared carefully and truthfully. Some reports do nothing but presenting information, while some others are analytical which include interpretation of data together with conclusions and recommendations. Reports are formal in writing style as well as in physical appearance. They are problem-solving. The problem must be clearly defined. The problem might be, for example, decline in sales, and in this, a report seeks to determine its causes. As the first step, a preliminary investigation is conducted and various factors are taken stock of. For this, the originality and purposefulness of a researcher are to be imbibed by report-writer. Most reliable information is to be collected from all imaginable sources. All the information thus collected is to be collated and logical, honest and unbiased analysis and interpretations are required to be effected with the help of various statistical tools. The writer must be very careful in reaching conclusions based on complete data only, and not on his premonitions. After organizing the information, the report writer makes-out his report in forthright and unambiguous manner. The style may generally be 'personal', since it is more forceful and direct than 'impersonal' type. The style should be selected depending on the requirements of the situation. The writer should write his report in an interesting manner; interesting writing is necessary for good communication.

Reports can be rendered orally too. An oral report is a presentation of factual information together with its interpretation orally. Oral and written reports are essentially of the same kind. In written communication, unlike in the oral, one can present facts in a wholesome manner and the reader is given adequate freedom to go through the written material at his own pace. There is little scope for effecting any possible corrections vis-à-vis grammar and composing style once the report is presented, unlike in the case of the oral. Even though thorough preparation is required in both the cases, written ones allow leisure and cool thinking before and during making of them, while in the case of the oral one, besides their absence, due to eye-contacts with the audience, the speaker is very likely to miss some of the subtle but important points and mar the free flow of information, barring stage fright and nervousness on the part of the speaker-presenter. Because of availability of instant feedback, the presenter gets a plus-one opportunity to correct factual errors crept-in inadvertently or iterate missed-out points and the like in his concluding words. There are no such opportunities in the case of written reports, as conclusion once written becomes permanent and inflexible or inelastic.

## Oral Communication

The use of oral communication applies to many areas—addressing a public meeting or company's board meeting, making presentation, communicating within or without groups and the like. Thus oral communication has two dimensions, first, communication within the organization and the second that with outsiders. As we have seen, communication within the organization can be upward, downward and lateral. It consists of face-to-face conversations, talks, speeches in conferences, meetings, telephonic and intercom conversations, video presentations, interviews, etc. This direct medium ensures physical proximity, instant interchange of opinions and instant feedback. Through this medium, it is easier to convince and persuade those who receive the messages. Incidentally, it is interesting to note that saying "No", emphatically or mildly, to someone on telephone is easier than in a face-to-face dialogue, obviously because of the absence of eye-contact. The face-to-face communication also ensures participation of all concerned and their direct contributions. It offers some disadvantages too. It is very difficult to hold ground in face of opposition. It is rather difficult to control the proceedings if the number of people attending is more; often disputes and discords might arise. Moreover, the quality of decision-making may be inferior. That is why most of the meetings end-up inconclusively. Chaos and confusions will be the end result. The second, communication with outsiders, i.e. with suppliers, service providers, customers and the general public. Business efforts by salesmen, interactions by those doing personal selling, telephone callbacks, follow-up service calls, and advertising efforts through radio are also included in it. All these are to be very cautiously executed; otherwise the resultant ramifications would be disastrous.

Like in written communication, the oral too will have an introduction, main body and conclusion. Subject is to be stated clearly in the introduction. The talk should have a suitable title which serves to indicate to the audience as to the theme of the talk and how much area that would be covered. He has to elicit interest and enthusiasm from the listeners. The main body should have points arranged in a logical order, with relevant arguments to support each point. In the conclusion, all important points covered earlier in the talk should be summarized and high-lighted. At the end of the talk, the speaker should have achieved in his effort to make the audience comprehend clearly the purpose of his talk and persuade them to follow his action plan. Some sporadic sprinkle of subtle humour relevant to the subject matter at appropriate situations will eliminate any cause of monotony and enhance attentiveness of the audience.

The following points are worth remembering:

(a) Adhere to time-element. Time to start and to finish to be strictly adhered to.
(b) Select a topic that interests the speaker, if choice is available. Play on a home ground.
(c) Provide reliable evidence to claims made by the speaker.
(d) Stand upright, balanced and relaxed.
(e) Establish eye-contact with each and every member of the audience.
(f) Do not fidget.
(g) The speaker should not read his speech.
(h) Suitable visuals will aid explanations.
(i) Speak up.
(j) Solicit questions and answer them convincingly.
(k) Ensure dynamics in delivery.

**Interviews**

An interview is a two-way interactive communication. Neither an interviewer nor an interviewee is doing a favour to each other. The interviewee is looking for a job and the employer is looking for someone suitable to fill a vacancy. In fact it is a mutual help. The candidate should present himself smartly and neatly dressed. He must be honest to himself while interacting with the interviewer. One should not forget that the interviewer has fair amount of information about the candidate through the letter of application. Most of the questions asked would be required to be answered in sentences, and not 'yes' or 'no'. Such questions are intended to test the candidate's communicating abilities. If one can express himself well, both in writing and in speech, and can look and sound pleasant, his chances to getting selected will be greatly increased.

## Effective Meetings

Meetings essentially are communicative interactions. Meetings are held between or among two or more individuals, coming together to discuss some common problems or interests and to arrive at sagacious solutions that will ultimately enhance the health of the organization that all of them represent. They can be 'formal' and 'informal'. In either case, their effectiveness can be measured in terms of the quality, clarity, economy of efforts and relevance of the result, and the speed with which questions are resolved and action taken. The two important requirements for effective meetings are that communication should take place in a free and orderly manner and that the content should be relevant. Hence the aim and relevance of the meeting must be clearly digested by those attending it, well before the timing and scheduling of the meeting are done. Only then can meetings be effective. Every participant should be prepared to listen to one another and consider the points covered and they should not be afraid of putting forward their own points, views and ideas, and thus ensuring their total involvement. Disagreements are not to be suppressed, but are not to be allowed to dominate to make a sort of 'tyranny of the minority'. Decisions are required to be arrived at by consensus.

## Communication Patterns in Groups

The main features are as follows:

(a) Information giving from central point to all others.

(b) Collecting information from participants.

(c) Decision-making by taking all information inputs into consideration.

(d) Explanation of decisions made.

(e) Problem solving.

Teleconference is another type of communication. It is the live exchange and mass articulation of information among persons and machines remote from one another but linked by a telecommunication system, usually over the phone lines. It differs from videophone in intending to serve groups rather than individuals. Teleconferences are also referred to as teleseminars. Alternative terms for teleconferencing include audio conferencing, telephone conferencing and phone conferencing.

**Taking Sides**

Partiality is a part of human communicating activity. We take sides in a discussion, a debate, an argument or a negotiation. Newspaper reporters and editors reflect bias in the emphasis they give to the virtues of one political party or political system, the government or trade unions, the North or the South, the East or the West and so on. Some newspapers and visual media do their best to report objectively, giving equal weight to both sides leaving the readers to form their own opinions and conclusions.

The undermentioned pairs of words are examples of emotive use of language. Emotions, of course, drive us to action, but at the same time cause us to search for contrary reasons as well, if we do not subscribe to any one of them.

'Terrorists' and 'freedom fighters',

'Diplomat' and 'trickster',

'Brave' and 'foolhardy',

'Business men' and 'robber',

'Loyal' and 'sycophantic',

'Colourful' and 'gaudy',

'Steadfast' and 'obstinate',

'Decorative' and 'pretentious',

'Baber mosque' and 'disputed structure'.

An appeal on behalf of the starving children or mistreated prisoners, for instance, is inevitably directed at the emotions, but may nonetheless be honest. The well-known speech by Mark Antony in *Julius Caesar* is a typical example of emotive communication. At times, emotive communication is used dishonestly as well. Such situations do arise everyday, in business as well as in private lives of individuals.

## Negotiations

Negotiation is an art. None can become a good negotiator merely following a set of rules, firstly because all personalities are different, and secondly because no one set of negotiations is quite like another; personalities, issues and circumstances are all different. So this art has to be studied and the skills carefully acquired. This skill can be successfully developed by experience.

## Steps in Negotiation

The various steps are as follows:

(a) Collecting information.

(b) Preparing of the case.

(c) Planning the strategy.

(d) Starting negotiation.

(e) Implementing the result.

The negotiator must collect all relevant accurate factual information about the subject to be negotiated. The subject in an industrial situation may be disputes pertaining to grievances of employees vis-a-vis the working environment or wage and bonus claims. If the dispute relates to grievances, then information regarding the people involved, exact nature of grievances and the like must be known and correctly understood by the negotiator. If the dispute relates to wage and bonus claims, then information about general cost of living and price index, productivity and profit generation, general economic health of the organization and the like must be known and correctly understood by the person entrusted with negotiation. It is always good to foresee and forecast the lines of argument or the strategies going to be adopted by the other side; so also their strong and weak areas, at the same time he should be able to anticipate adverse arguments or alternative suggestions from the other side.

It is a well-known fact that information and knowledge make one confident. After collecting relevant information from all sources, the negotiator must ascertain by effecting sedulous scrutiny the veracity of each piece of it. He then will have to study, analyse and collate all the information. Preparation for negotiation is like that of a war. In the game of cricket, to bring-in an analogy, every batsman 'going out into the middle' aims at a 'century', but he may or may not perform accordingly as he wanted. There could be a gap between what one hopes to achieve and what one actually does. Before the actual process of negotiation takes off, it is better to decide what one hopes to gain and what he is willing to concede, and ensure that demands and suggestions are within reasonable limits.

Next step is consideration of strategy. Strategy must be planned in advance, and the timing is important. Bargaining should be done when the other side is weakest. The most favourable time will differ according to the company, industry and the economy. A trade union, for instance, should not plan on being tough when there is high degree of unemployment. It is better to think out the consequences of various types of approach and settlement. Never try to 'pull a fast one'; one should think optimistically that the strategy planned will stand on its own merits. Deception or sharp dealings might bring about temporary advantage or gain, but in the long run it will create suspicion and loss of credibility. One must remember that it is all a psychological warfare.

Once the strategy is outlined, actual negotiation can start. There are mainly three steps in the process. They are as follows:

(a) All matters on which agreement can be reached are to be treated settled, lest one should waste time and temper on unnecessary details. This first step is exploratory.

(b) The negotiator should go through all the proposals; listen carefully and watch reactions of the other side.

(c) It is not advisable to keep 'all cards open' at the outset itself; keep some 'close to the chest' and keep 'something up the sleeve'.

The following points are some general guidelines:

(1) Adjourn to consider new proposals or counter proposals.

(2) Do not think loudly.

(3) Review discussion after revising plan.

(4) Do not get bogged down in prolonged discussion over minor items.

(5) Find out points of disagreement—how much serious are they?

(6) Good listening.

(7) Remember context in which words and phrases used.

(8) Evaluate intent of the other party and explore flaws in argument.

(9) Avoid contradicting team members.

(10) Brief and business-like approach.

(11) Wherever possible, be hard as diamond and at the same time as soft as a flower.

(12) Toughness versus noisiness.

(13) Avoid lung power and bad temper.

(14) Be courteous.

(15) Look for changes in stances and attitudes of other side, adapt to change.

(16) Provide 'escape route' to other side, as a part of strategy.

(17) Be persuasive and compromising.

(18) Prioritization.

(19) Re-wording proposals.

(20) Decide minimum settlements acceptable.

(21) Do not concede simply for settlement.

Details of all the decisions arrived at, during the process of negotiation, must be brought on written record in unambiguous and succinct manner. There should be *consensus ad idem* between both the sides. Before the deliberations conclude, it is of paramount importance to recapitulate the points of decisions in presence of both the sides. This record must be signed and copies held by both sides. All the terms of the settlement are to be implemented, and periodical 'follow-up' reviews conducted in this respect.

**Feedback**

We have seen that in any organization, individuals working together interact formally or informally between and among them on their feelings, impressions and views on various matters. This is intrinsically thus a process of inter-personal transaction. The receiver conveys his perception, with regard to the message he received, to the sender. Consider the fact that this transaction is between two individuals, although it happens in a group. The feedback is not merely a communication of the perception of the receiver but it is intended to establish an understanding and a trusted relationship between two individuals. If these are healthy, then the organization will be ultimately benefited. In the case of oral communication, the feedback is fairly instant in the form of gleaming of eyes, nod of his head or the general body language. A watchful sender will be able to take instant corrective action if the feedback he receives is not in conformity with what he expected, whereas in written communication, as the feedback is not instant, he has to be more careful at the time of sending the message. On the other hand, if these are unhealthy, there will be a number of problems that can adversely affect the overall efficiency and effectiveness of the organization. The result of these interactions provides many vital inputs to the management. The management can use it profitably, if it is positive. The negative ones enable it to effect necessary adjustments and changes in the course of its functioning. Feedback is thus a vital ingredient in all types and modes of communication.

A feedback *per se* is a communication, taking place in the reverse order. Hence it too has all the ingredients of any outgoing communication. Hence the receiver has to address all those ingredients while initiating his feedback message and ensure that these are taken care of, because here the receiver and the sender interchange their role and status. A system of feedback serves as a set of mirrors that reflect and reveal the personality traits of the sender as well as the receiver. Feedback offers an opportunity to either of them to introspect and evaluate the relevance and effectiveness of either of them, as sender and receiver.

# 3

# Use of Proverbs, Sayings, Idioms and Phrases in Communication

The language of English can be thought of in two forms, namely, Correct English and Good English. Correct English is the one with full attention, adherence and stress to the principles of Grammar of the language, and Good English is the one with various expressions incorporated therein, enhancing the beauty of the language. Good English too would be Correct English. Correct English *per se* may not be beautiful and usually is abstract in nature. It is like pure mathematics, where two plus two is four, whereas Good English is like its applied version where two plus two would be made to look as more or less than four. Good English is impregnated with usages of appropriate proverbs, sayings, idioms and phrases to evince emotional ethos, thus rendering it more effective and appealing. Hence the importance of Good English in Communication, written or oral, need not be overemphasized.

Proverbs, sayings, idioms and phrases are purposely employed in communication, written or oral in order to bring home great ideas substantiating points of view. A proverb is a short familiar sentence expressing a supposed truth or moral lesson; a maxim, a general principle, serving as a rule or guide. It is a dispensation in condensed or compressed form of great expressions, conveying much more than it appears to contain.

One can expand and interpret each of them and make out a treatise. It is a sort of effective human communication, employing minimum number of words with maximum meaning. They are used in every language. Proverbs determine actions and emotions. Some of them are expressions of hope, fatalism, cynicism and consolation. The following are a few of the examples:

(1) The darkest hour is that before the dawn. (2) Man proposes, God disposes. (3) Many would be cowards if they had courage enough. (4) Marry in haste, repent in leisure. (5) Spare the rod and spoil the child. (6) What can't be cured must be endured.

Some of the popular proverbs and their connotations in brief are given below:

1. Caught between the devil and the deep blue sea (to be stuck with two choices that are both undesirable).
2. Out of the frying pan and into the fire (to go from a bad to a worse situation).
3. Might as well be hanged for a sheep as a lamb (if you're going to get into the same amount of trouble, you might as well commit the greater offense).
4. Six of one, half a dozen of the other (each choice is really the same thing).
5. Two sides of the same coin (two aspects of a situation that are connected by necessity).
6. In for a penny, in for a pound (if you're going to make a minor commitment you might as well make the entire commitment).
7. Don't count your chickens before they're hatched (don't start making plans for something until it is a reality, rather than a pleasant speculation).
8. Don't cross your bridges before you get to them (don't worry about future problems before you need to).

9. A stitch in time saves nine (if you take care of a problem while it's small you won't have a bigger problem to deal with later).
10. Time and tide wait for none (act in a timely fashion because you can't get back lost chances).

Proverbs, sayings, idioms and phrases do not appear abruptly all of a sudden; they are not created by anyone's design; they are evolved out of popular wisdom of mankind cultured over the ages. They are time-tested proven and accepted universally.

A proverb when employed in any type of communication, written or oral, can minimize the use of words and at the same time ideas can be conveyed more effectively and efficiently. Only a person with developed mind and thorough knowledge of situations can effectively employ proverbs. He would have command over the language. William Shakespeare coined many a proverbial phrase. He contributed to or popularized more phrases and sayings in the English language than any other individual and most of them are still in daily use. A few of them among the hundreds are cited below:

**Sayings**

(1) A rose by any other name would smell as sweet. (2) All that glitters is not gold. (3) All is well that ends well. (4) Discretion is the better part of valour. (5) Fight fire with fire. (6) Frailty, thy name is woman. (7) Give the devil his due.

**Phrases**

(1) A fool's paradise. (2) Vanish into thin air. (3) A foregone conclusion. (4) A sea change. (5) As good luck would have it. (6) Beware the ides of March. (7) Come what may. (8) Ettu, Brute. (9) Good riddance. (10) Heart's content.

Proverbs have great utility in the realm of learning and education. Children in their early years of learning use proverbs not only to improve their handwriting but also develop their intellect. Hence, they form a vital component of courses for learning languages. More importantly, understanding the meaning of proverbs provides the real challenge for students at all levels.

Several groups of students with the same levels of physical and intellectual age can be formed as participants of a workshop wherein they are told to read, understand and memorize a large number of proverbs and to engage themselves in conversing among themselves only through these proverbs. Two students A and B are told to engage themselves in such an exercise wherein B is told to provide proverbs with similar meanings as those of what A would be coming-up with. For example:

A. Make hay while the sun shines. B. Never put off till tomorrow what may be done today.

A. One of these days is none of these days. B. Opportunity seldom knocks twice.

A. Strike while the iron is hot. B. There is no time like the present. The group can be told to fill up blanks. For example:

1 ......... when most needed is least heeded. (Advice)
2. Better to ask the way than go.......... (astray)
3. A contented mind is a perpetual......... (feast)
4. Discontent is the first step in......... (progress)
5. Idle folk have the least......... (leisure)
6. Virtue is its own......... (reward)
7. Out of sight, out of......... (mind)

There are some proverbs prescribing certain meanings; but there are some others that connote opposite meanings. Both of them are equally relevant. Let us examine the following sets:

1. A bird in the hand is worth two in the bush. A man's reach should exceed his grip.
2. Clothes make the man. Never judge a book by its cover.
3. Doubt is the beginning of wisdom. Faith will move mountains.
4. Silence is golden. Only the crying child gets milk.

5. You are never too old to learn. You cannot teach an old dog new tricks.
6. The pen is mightier than the sword. Actions speak louder than words.
7. Wise men think alike. Fools seldom differ.

There are proverbs indicating impossibilities or improbabilities like:

Trying to grow lotus plant on dry land.

Trying to straighten the canine tail.

Asking a blind person to look into a mirror.

Taking a horse to water and forcing it to drink.

An idiom is a mode of expression, not logically or grammatically explicable, characteristic of a particular language. Idioms and the phrases are groups of words have similar functions to perform. Unlike in the case of many of the phrases, idioms have usually indirect implied and indicative connotations and relevance to the context in which they are employed. Most of the phrases have direct and open explanations. Many of the idioms are formed from parts of some proverbs or sayings. There is great use of figures of speech in idiomatic expressions unlike in phrases. Some of the examples of idiomatic phrases are given below:

> Cook the accounts; on the fence; dig heels in; walls have ears; once in a while; get into an argument; sad state of affairs; make a fuss; fool's paradise; thin end of a wedge, etc.

Since all of these proverbs, sayings and idioms form an integral part of any language and literature, it is imperative that anyone should master the art and skill of employing them carefully, judiciously and freely in his writing or speaking practices.

# 4

# Soliloquy—A Sort of Communication

Soliloquy is also a sort of communication. Every person thinks, some silently and some others 'loudly'. Thinking *per se* is 'silent soliloquy'. People do not generally make any audible voices or noises while thinking. They do not offer or manifest any visible symptom or proof of the working of their 'internal cumbustion engines (ICEs'). No 'smoke' or 'heat' is allowed to be emitted from these ICEs. Some people, in some cases, on the other hand, give out indicative clues or cues; they 'talk in sign language' using their lips, teeth, eyes, nose, heads, fingers, shoulders, hands and legs by different gestures, unaware of or ignoring of surroundings. It is an unconscious automatic pressure relieving system. More often, it serves to prepare oneself to meet some impending eventuality, mostly unpleasant and unwelcome ones. He looks around involuntarily and ascertains that none is present in the vicinity in the visible zone, or in the audible range, and then he 'discusses' all his personal problems loudly with himself. The moment someone appears abruptly in front of him, he stops his performance, soliloquising. When he is confronted with an enquiry as to what has he been talking to himself all alone, he denies his having said anything; he would clarify that he has only been thinking about a particular vexing problem faced by him then.

I saw a person, looking-upward aimlessly, and uttering something, sometimes angrily and sometimes laughingly, mostly in lowly audible voice, but sometimes in highly audible manner. It seemed that his 'speech' was directed to certain invisible person. I was standing nearby and observing him, but out of his visible or audible range, even though he was, with respect to me. My inquisitiveness propelled me towards him, and immediately on seeing me, he stopped his 'speech' and started gazing upwards, donning an expression of contempt on his face towards this unwelcome disturbing intruder. I ventured to confront him with my enquiry as to whom and what was he talking about. "Nothing. Are you joking or dreaming? Are you mad or am I?" was his reply. Armed with sufficient convincing foolproof evidence against him, giving no escape route, I confronted him again. His adamancy waned and hesitatingly confessed of his having said something all alone. "You see that cob-web up there. I was thinking about that. Don't you also think always on something? I also do the same. The difference is that when you think you do not speak out anything, whereas I speak out when and what I think. Probably I do not have any 'clutch-and-gear-system' built-in to curb this. Hence I talk what I think about." The reply was quite logical and satisfactory. He is a patient of schesophrania. He was trying cleverly to hoodwink me by telling that he was thinking about the cob-web. He was in fact having someone in his mind at that time, and was talking to and discussing with that invisible person. This is soliloquy of one kind probably due to some bitter haunting experience in life which might have caused melacholy, depression and obsession. It is 'communication with a difference'; it is communication with one's own self—soliloquy. It could be an effort to taking refuge from melancholy, working-out strategies for escapade from unpleasantness or make it serve as pressure relieving measures.

On the other hand, if he does not stop his soliloquising and chooses not to answer any question, others have every right to declare him of unsound mind. Anger, curses, hatred, worries, sorrows, grievances, depression, frustrations, unhappiness and other negative feelings go diluted and dissipated by this process. He could be weeping at times. Happiness, good wishes and other positive elements of sentiments too become subject matter of soliloquy. Enhancement of these positive sentiments finds expression in the form of smiling and laughing, sometimes even boisterously, which may, though rarely, be indicative of pitying or condemning oneself or others; or self-enjoyment. We oberve that when someone initiates a good joke and served to a less intelligent person, the latter laughs boisterously after the lapse of some time. Here the whole process consumes some time. We often compare the behaviour of such persons to that of fluorescent lamps. This demeanour of these people does in no way indicate that they had engaged themselves in soliloquising before they laughed. Imaginative people are more prone to soliloquising. People often see persons in inebriated condition and resort to soliloquising. Nevertheless, it is all communication of some sort.

In the context of dramatics, speech, words or sentences addressed to the speaker himself, disregardful of or oblivious to any hearer present is called a soliloquy. Soliloquy is used in plays to great advantage. It is very effective in order to reveal the thoughts, emotions and motives of various characters without resorting to narration by a third person. The great playwright Shakespeare used this soliloquy effectively in many of his plays like *Macbeth* and *Hamlet*. The soliloquy is clearly delivered and can be heard only by the audience. The other characters on the stage are presumed not to be hearing or noticing what is happening. In contrast, a monologue is a speech addressed to another person or group of persons. Sometimes a speech addressed to an absent character is also called a monologue. Various characters in plays do rehearsing their spoken parts alone in their 'green rooms' as for preparation. These are addressed to themselves to build-up confidence in themselves before the actual delivery on the stage. This is neither soliloquy nor monologue in *absentia* of the characters they have in mind. It has, however, a semblance of communication, though in conventional sense, it may not have.

# 5

# Silence—A Mode of Communication

Silence is an unused tool that is very effective in all kinds of situations. Silence is nothingness. More than half of Beethoven's music is silence. Without the silence there is no music, there is only noise. It is peacefulness. Silence is a widely-known, but rarely used, powerful communicating tool. Utilizing the 'sound' of silence is truly an ultimate in the art of communication. It is spiritually and socially acceptable passive assertiveness. The ability to remain quiet confirms that one is in total control of oneself. It also confirms that the individual is disciplined and will not be led into conversations that are counterproductive and energy-draining. Silence speaks volumes. There is always time to talk and there is always time to be silent. Silence is not the absence of communication. The more one speaks, the more mistakes he is likely to commit. It is paradoxical, but true, when we say that silence makes the greatest 'noise'. Some of the great orators do not speak continuously; they give intermittent pauses, in between important words or sentences. These pauses make their audience fill-up these 'temporary vacancies' with their own words. If the orator speaks the same words in due course as they had used for filling-up, the audience gets thrilled. This will enable the speaker to buy their attentiveness and carry his audience along. The audience gets charged-up, and heartily accepts the points of view of the speaker. Some teachers while teaching leave some sentences incomplete for the students to complete them. This is to buy their attentiveness.

Heat of arguments in a group gets 'deflated' or dissipated by this great tool called silence. In the world of communication, silence often sends a powerful message. Not saying a word in certain situations speaks volumes, whether it is in a presentation, a negotiation, a heated debate or argument with a co-worker or family member. If one is asked a question and he does not immediately respond or hesitate to respond, it could communicate many things. He could be thinking, angry, uncomfortable or just not sure what he wants to say in response. He could also be avoiding, belittling or deriding the person who had asked the question. In the Indian context, in rural conservative social set-up, if an eligible handsome bachelor confronts an eligible attractive spinster with some simple harmless questions, the latter chooses to keep silent even though she knows the answers. This silence of hers is taken for sign of shyness or even of aristocracy on her part. The dictum, "For every question, there shall be an answer" is flouted in this case. This is a value addition ploy employed by the great Manipulator, Nature.

Silence can be employed by a speaker to intimidate and dominate his audience. It helps one as a communicator to pace oneself and breathe. It allows him to organize his thoughts and emphasize one point or another. It builds anticipation in his audience and allows them to follow his message. Let me cite an example. On the very next day of the declaration of National Emergency in India the daily newspapers were published blank without a word. It was in protest against curb and gag on the media. It could convey many things. We are very used to constant sound. We need to learn to see silence or pausing as similar to the "white space" in a print advertisement in a newspaper, magazine or billboard. Too many words without enough "white space" can bring-in monotony and cause a message to be lost. The same thing is true of spoken words. Pausing and silence create the "white space" to put those words in context. Hence one of the most important parts of any conversation is the silence. Silence can serve many functions in a conversation; how one would manage it determines his level of sophistication. Silence serves as an indicator of wisdom. Allowing silence in a conversation puts pressure on the other person. Silence can indicate hostility, disagreement, respect, contemplation and rudeness. It can be creation of a listening space. It can also be an indication of empathy. How one manages silence in conversation is an important part in the overall context of emotional intelligence.

When one experiences anger, fear, or embarrassment, one's thinking brain shuts down. He sits there fuming, unable to speak; enraged and unable to find words; scared and speechless. Sometimes when one is listening to someone else, he hears something that leaves him speechless because it really goes beyond words. Listening to someone's talk about a dreadful trauma he has endured, or a beautiful or almost-sacred interaction with another human being or a description of an awesome natural event such as a sunset or a volcanic eruption could be examples. Somehow when he listens to such things, the ordinary "Oh"s and "Wow"s don't seem enough, and so he falls silent. In some cultures, silence indicates respect. A young person may be expected to approach an older person or a person in authority and remain silent until recognized, acknowledged and spoken to. The more introverted one's communication partner, the more likely he will think before he speaks. Extroverts discover what they are thinking and how they feel by talking. Introverts figure it all out inside their own head and heart before giving voice to it.

Silence can mean intentional rudeness. Refusing to reply to the other person is a way of ignoring him. Some students sitting silent in the first row of seats in the classroom or innocent farmers sitting in front of the podium attending election speech by some prominent politician encourage the teacher or the politician, as the case may be, by different non-verbal means, like nodding of heads synchronizing with different accents of the speaker, donning occasional smile, allowing eyes to gleam and eye-brows to move up-and-down in agreement and appreciation of the content of the speech, conveying a "you-are-great" message, and the like. All these expressions may not be genuine always, but they are silently communicative. Excellent communicators can allow silence when it's effective or called for; can avoid being pressured into "spilling" when silence is used manipulatively; offer silence as a gift or sign of respect; interpret the silence of others appropriately; understand how other cultures use silence; mindfully regulate the use of silence; and are comfortable with silence and understand its many uses.

There is an interesting fact. We have observed as to how shepherds talk to their cattle. In fact, these are not mere talking, they do 'discuss' with them on many issues like prevailing weather conditions, availability of water in the vicinity, the beauty of the meadows, exultations and sorrows and everything except probably prevailing political situations in the world. These are "deemed" two-way communications, as there are, at least, imaginary responses from the cattle, in the form of body language involving their heads and eyes.

The shepherds seem to get (or imagine to get) adequate responses to their queries from the cattles. In fact, these cattle are conditioned by the reiterations of the same matter by the shepherd many a time, and because of this they might be coming to know the gist of these messages through a latent and presumed stimulus-response system. Similarly, in rural settings, people foster and treat cattle as part of their household. They are housed in special cattle sheds and are cared for and given status of members of their household. Each one of them is christened by human names. In response to the "mewing" of one of the cows, someone would shout from inside the house, "Rita, I know what you want. I am coming bringing it. Wait." The cow stops mewing and awaits the arrival of the kind master. Here in this case, the cow, the sender, has sent its message to its master, the receiver; the receiver got the message right and sent his response, and the cow received an instant positive feedback from the receiver. The original as well as the feedback messages transmitted have been clear and devoid of any corruptions or confusion. An effective two-way communication has thus been consummated. Similarly, a lot of conversations and discussions take place between the cow and the lady-milkier during progression of the milking-process. The subjects include the ill-health of the granny of their house, marriage of the young lady in the house, scarcity of green grass in the vicinity, elopement of the young maid-domestic servant along with the neighbour-lover boy and the like. It seems that these are topics of their common interest! An on-looker might conclude that the milkier is insane. The cattle seem to notice and empathize with the sorrows and smiles of their masters and understand their body as well as the 'stick' languages. The masters reciprocate empathy received by them from their 'wards'.

It may not be sheer imagination when we say that there exists a subtle communication system between a child in the womb and its potential mother. It is known fact that the mother unconsciously conveys through the nerves network, blood, genes, food supplies and even breath, her feelings of happiness, unhappiness, fear and anxieties experienced by her during pregnancy, to the foetus growing within her. That is why there is a platitude that the expectant mothers should be kept happy and cheerful always in order to ensure that the children born would be mentally and physically healthy.

It is imaginative to believe that protons and electrons in an atom, staying 'separately' in a spatial arrangement of energy levels, communicate with each other. "We are together to form a unit. I am aware that we have no separate lives. We complement each other. But for our common good, we have to live separately, yet together. We have to maintain our status as separate individuals lest we should perish. You stay there only and perform your part of the duty, while I stay in my place and do mine. Be happy," the protons tell the electrons. "We agree" is their response, and they maintain some natural equilibrium. And they cohabit as an ideal wed-lock similar to that of human beings. It is good for both the human spouses to adopt this philosophy. And those who do not adopt it, it might be difficult for them to save their marriage. Similar is the case with the solar system, the macrocosm, wherein some sort of interactions on the same lines take place between the sun and its planets; between and among the planets; between and among the planets and their moons; among the whole of the solar family, all together forming-up a web. All these have semblance of 'a network of communication'.

It is interesting to note that some sort of communication takes place between dreamers and their fortunate or unfortunate 'victims'. It is very difficult, if not impossible, to say a "NO" or a lie to another person who does not want to receive a negative response when both of them establish eye contact in a direct face-to-face interaction. Some people resort to closing their eyes while conveying such things even in direct interactions, like cats do while drinking milk stealthily, imagining that none sees the act of commission of the offence and avoiding getting caught 'red-handed' and punished. Most of the times cats are successful; but some day or sometimes the 'cat would be out'. Such people might resort to giving excuses for their 'inabilities' which, save first one or two occasions, turn out to be untruths; untruths are seldom bought. Such people are of diffident personality or hypocrites. The best channel of communication on such occasions would be the telephonic one. It is easy to do so in dreams as well. In dreams cowards and those who are afraid of 'facing facts' have a field day. Dream communication is resorted to convey positive messages too. Lovers too resort to dream communication to convey "I love you" to their love when face-to-face or telephonic or telepathic means is insufficient to serve their cause. Communication via dreams is a 'safe bet' in all these cases. It is a 'mostly' a silent communication.

# 6

# Communication System in Military Context

System of communication prevalent between and among the personnel in military organizations is essentially the same as that exists in any of its civilian counterparts. Both the civil and military organizations consist of human beings working together with the sole goal of achieving their respective organizational objectives. The objectives of the military vary very much vis-à-vis those of business establishments; the military is unconcerned about the profit generation or its maximization which is the main concern for business establishments. But both the organizations, however, endeavour to achieve their respective objectives in the most effective, efficient and economical manner with the help of human beings, forming similar hierarchical echelons. Communication is of paramount importance in both these organizations.

"A leader is a person who influences a group to follow the course of action he advocates." A leader is always identified with the group of which he forms a part. It is his usual role to attempt to influence, and it is the followers' role to follow. The followers accept the formal leader's ideas, because the leader has authority over them. He dispenses rewards and punishments. Influence based on threats of punishment is not likely to be lasting. The followers will obey orders only so long as the led fear getting caught. It can be compared to the disciplined and orderly behaviour of an iron piece kept in a magnetic field; so long as it is in that field. The moment the field is removed, the iron piece behaves in its own way. Thus, such a leadership is neither effective nor long lasting. A leader's influence is not derived from an explicit position of authority. More than anything else, the group follows him, because his personal qualities convince them that they can satisfy their own needs by accepting his ideas. They truly believe in his ideas. For this to happen, the members of the group must be unsure of how to attain their goals on their own, and therefore they turn to the leader for achieving them. But how has he become the leader? Probably, one reason why the group relies on him is because of his past performance record. The second reason could be that he is most-liked and popular. A third could be that he is assertive. A leader is the 'tallest' member in a group. He commands respect due to his superiority in intelligence, knowledge, expertise, sagacity, kind-heartedness, transparency in dealings, honesty, impartiality and exemplary behaviour.

A leader does not function in a vacuum. He has got to carry his people with him always. An efficient leader must always give positive feedback to enthuse his people. Of course, negative feedback also has to be received and given, but a positive one produces positive results. "The day soldiers stop bring you their problems is the day you have stopped leading them" said General Colin Powell.

Leadership, to be able to achieve organizational effectiveness, has to inspire people. Philosophically speaking, a leader who can practise fearlessness, selfless work, universal love, perfect congruence between his thoughts and actions, makes himself an integrated human being. Effective leaders seem to be sensitive and thereby pay enough attention to people, their morale, organizational culture, fostering right kind of values and attitudes in them, providing avenues for development of their competence, and channelling their energies in the right directions. The manager or leader must ascertain for himself if his philosophy and style percolate down the line. He should devise means to know if he is paying adequate attention to 'softer dimensions' or the leadership he provides results in the optimum utilization of resource potential and thereby ensuring organizational effectiveness.

An officer in the armed forces is thus a manager, a leader, a teacher and a guide to his men. He has missions and objectives to be achieved for his organization during peace or war times. He achieves them with the help and support of his men. He elicits these through proper clear communicative interactions with his men. He can not afford to be away from his men psychologically even if not physically. He has to identify himself with the group he leads. He is a trainer and must be at constant pains to keep his troops abreast of all the latest tactical experience and developments, and must insist on their practical application. He must see to it that his subordinates are trained in accordance with the latest requirements. The best form of welfare for the troops is first-class training, for, this saves unnecessary casualties. A good training programme has great motivational potential; it is enhancing morale of his men.

In order, therefore, to lead effectively, the leaders, the military officers in this context, must be good communicators. If there is any ambiguity in conveying ideas and orders to their people, it will create confusion and misunderstandings and the resultant loss of an important campaign, offensive or defensive.

The main forms and systems of communication in the military organizations are as follows:

(a) **Loose Notes:** These are used for intra-formation communication to ensure co-ordination of the various activities between and among different sections and subsections within small formations. A standard lay-out is used in the whole of the military set-ups.

(b) **Formal Letters:** These are meant for inter-formation communication to ensure, again, co-ordination. These letters also serve to share information between and among sister formations as well as with their group headquarters or service headquarters as two-way communications. The group or service headquarters send policy matters and instructions on various operational and administrative matters through these letters. Lower formations use them to forward compliance reports and to seek advice on various matters. These are used between and among service headquarters under the Defence Ministry as well. A standard layout is used within the whole of the military set-ups.

(c) **Signal Communication:** This form in all respects is similar to communication by formal letters. Telecommunication and electronic facilities are used. 'Signals', as they are called, are nothing but a sort of 'telegrams' being sent on matters mainly on operational matters requiring expeditious actions. Messages containing classified information are sent after converting the contents into coded language, for obvious reasons, and sent out as ordinary signals. Replies received are decoded. Signal communication is done through tele-printers as well. Standard layouts and procedures are clearly laid down.

(d) **Demi-Official Letters:** These are the ones between two officials who have good personal understanding, rapport and friendliness between them. Such letters deal with official matters taken-up in personal level in order to elicit personal attention of the addressee and thereby seeking speedy treatment. They cut across hierarchical levels. It is an effective tool.

(e) **Informal Letters:** These are used for correspondence with civilian organizations. For urgent matters, civil telegrams are sent.

(f) **Communication between the Military and the Government:** It takes place in another special way. Formats used are different.

Existence and sustenance of military organizations as such are due to its ardent sense of discipline fastidiously integrated into their very system. It, however, does not mean that discipline is not a requirement in any of the civilian organizations. It is not my endeavour to dwell upon in detail the importance of discipline in the military, as it is beyond the scope of this treatise. Discipline, in military context, has two aspects—physical and mental, both affecting the communicative behaviour of the people involved. The body language itself is standardized due to strict discipline. It manifests itself in the physical training like marching in step, running, saluting and the like in physical training. These are expressions of behaviour that are understood by one and all alike without any ambiguity and misinterpretation. It is surprising to see that each member thinks alike and because of this their responses to stimuli, actions and reactions too will be standardized. All these contribute to building-up *esprit de corps*, the quintessential element required for success of any group activity, especially vis-à-vis military organizations. Inculcation of the sense of discipline brings forth a sort of conditioning, and this facilitates process of communication.

The written and even spoken communications too are standardized. They are designed to be concise, clear and to the point. For an outsider, many of the expressions employed in the spoken language in vogue in military organizations will sound very impolite and unkindly. This is merely a perceptual problem on the part of the outsider. There exists always a tinge of commanding flavour latent in whatever they speak. None in the military set-up is aware or conscious of it and none minds it, as all individuals are conditioned to transact that way. To cite a case in point, while on the 'marching parade', it is not enough for an officer 'to tell' his subordinates in a requesting tone, 'please turn to your right', to elicit an appropriate response from them. It is common knowledge that a 'request' or an 'advice' may be acceded to or rejected, at will, by the recipient of the request or advice. There is no binding. The parading column may not 'turn to the right' as 'requested' by the officer who might have to accomplish a military task or obligation. This *lissez faire* behaviour on the part of the officer as well as the soldiers might not be enough to accomplish the objective. So he would have to 'say', nay, 'shout' "RIGHT TURN" in a commanding tone instead of telling in an entreating manner, "Please turn to your right (*s'il vous plait*) or (if you don't mind)". All of them turn to their right mechanically instantaneously. They are not given any time to think or analyse the reasons why they are asked to turn to the right. "Why we should turn to the right?, why not to the left?, why at all we turn to any side?" or any other questions will have no relevance and hence they are neither thought of nor asked. They all accept such behaviour as an inevitable part of military life. This is a culture that is being handed down by generations to successive generations. They all form part of tradition. All members are proud of these traditions. Is this 'feeling proud' also due to a conditioning effect? Are they instructed to consider such things as traditions and to feel proud of, as part of conditioning?

A colonel was addressing his men in one of the routine welfare conclaves. As he could not afford to speak to them in his usual authoritarian style in such conclaves, he had many rehearsals on polite speaking style, on the quite, in his bungalow. He was quite successful at it till the end of his address. During the course of his speech, he 'entreated' his men to watch a magic show to be conducted by some magician, inside the camp premises at a subsidized price. "My boys, I have seen it. It is very good. I recommend that all of you should see it. There is no compulsion. But I strongly recommend it." Then he continued dealing with other matters. At the end of the speech, he got up from his seat and said, "Gentlemen, I hope you remember about the magic show which I had recommended. You all must see it. It is an ORDER."

# PART II

# 7

# Telepathy, Intuition and Instincts vis-à-vis Communication

Communication forms the quintessential ingredient for societal existence. There are various ways through which people communicate with each other. They manage it by tongue, teeth, mouth, nose, eyes, face, head, shoulders, hands, legs, whole body, laughing, dancing, weeping, touching and even by silence. In short, they use all the resources at their command for the purpose of communication. They share their ideas and emotions, actions and reactions through this communication with other members of the society.

Communication is nothing but a response to stimulus from either side. Plants and animals too engage themselves in communicating with each other. A 'touch-me-not' plant, for example, responds the moment anyone touches it, by folding all of its leaves spontaneously, to scare away its 'enemy'. We have known about how carnivorous plants behave. If any one catches hold of the tail of a donkey, the stimulus; it gives a back-kick, the response to that stimulus. These are examples of the ways of communication among flora and fauna.

Human beings communicate with their fellow beings with their minds as well. This is what we call 'telepathy'. There are some prerequisites for establishing mind-to-mind communication system between two persons. Both of them should be having the same 'wavelength' of thoughts and opinions in the various fields of psychology, philosophy, physiology and parity in their standing in the society they belong to. That is to say, both of them should have similar living conditions and they face common or similar problems in their day-to-day lives. They maintain an ideal and never failing friendship and mutual understanding.

There should be mutual admiration between them and for that they should be of good character and demeanour. Thus, we have two identical minds whose mutual mental vibrations resonate. To state the least, sympathy as well as empathy for each other is another requisite. They should have unquestionable mutual love and respect, and share identical feelings about their enemies, if any. Mostly, they have common enemies in the form of human beings or untenable philosophical concepts. Above all, they have had immense interactions during their very long association in their lives, as though they have been cohabiting. This is a beautiful situation, a congenial atmosphere for telepathy.

Geographic distances do not concern telepathists. They can communicate even if they are separated by thousands of kilometres. They never go 'out of range'. If they happen to meet each other, telepathy gets short-circuited, and no words will be required to convey any message. They both look at a person, an object or a situation and probably smile at each other after establishing eye-contact. Their smile and eye-contact mutually convey whole lot of their impressions within seconds. This is the fastest mode of communication, at no-cost-basis. In case of wireless communication, it is slower, a bit more expensive, at the same time messages could get corrupted too. *Consensus ad idem* is the motto of any communication and it is achieved totally in telepathy. When their eyes meet, they exchange or share volumes of information within microseconds, without uttering a word. Their 'tell-tale' smiles convey everything without any ambiguity.

Telepathic abilities may become weakened or subdued if the persons concerned do not maintain constant continual touch, physical or mental, for a long duration of time. Our mobile telephones do not work properly or stop working at all, if the battery goes weak or unserviceable. Battery needs re-charging and is to be kept in serviceable condition at all times, and cannot be re-charged once it becomes 'life expired'. But in case of telepathy its 'battery' does not totally go 'life-expired', and some residual life will be left behind, and as such, can be rejuvenated. Once the contacts are re-established, either physically or mentally, telepathic system will be re-instated without more ado.

Intuition *per se* is not communication; but it is a motive force for it. Intuition expresses itself in terms of actions, non-actions and reactions, positive or negative; all these culminate in communication. Intuition reflects power of the mind by which it immediately perceives the truth of things without reasoning or analysis. The incidence of this phenomenon, it appears, is the result of some unknown or imperceptible programming in the brain brought-in by some unknown agency or indelible inherited impressions imprinted on the brain. Incredible. Intuition comes about impulsively, leaving behind no overt evidence of pre-meditation or deliberate design. Intuition and instinct are 'born twins' with identical features. Instincts are involuntary prompting actions; the mental aspects of theirs take rank between unconscious reflex activities and intelligent conduct. The natural impulse is independent of reason or experience.

Let us take-up two cases of actions by a two-year old child while he is playing in the open. In the first case, he is seen playing with snails and worms. The child has no idea of what these are. Sometimes if the child is hungry or even as a fancy takes one of them and devours, without knowing the consequences or after effects of such an action. There is no ostentatious role for instinct or intuition in this. The child develops vomiting sensation, stomach upset or fever due to a possible infection, but the child does not have any clue of what has happened to him. He does not even learn anything from this experience at that age to protect himself from any such things in future. In the second case, the child plays with a scorpion. Here he gets punished, and probably, earns a deterring effect. He may not go near a scorpion in future. He might develop fear psychosis. In the second case, it is probable that he has for himself developed some sort of instinct or intuition. So some previous experience comes into play as minimum requirement for developing either instinct or intuition.

Intuition springs out from accumulated effects or impressions from past experiences kept 'saved' in one's brain-computer. The moment an individual faces a problematic situation, a matching solution is served out to him readily available 'ex-stock' from his already 'saved' assets in his brain. This we call instinct or intuition. Intuitionalism is a doctrine that envisages that perception of truth is by intuition. There is apparently no room for exercising sense of reasoning or analysis. Everything happens unconsciously and instantaneously and that is why we reckon it as a semblance of an automatic programming of some sort in the brain.

All members of the fauna are bestowed with the tool of instinct. All human beings too behave instinctively and intuitively. A woman, a mother, was travelling sitting in a train. She was holding her one-year-old child in her lap. In the dead of the night the child was, as usual, asleep and the mother too was helplessly feeling very sleepy, and succumbed. Even the slightest of the jerks or disturbance in the compartment would make her hold the child tight, even while she was continuing with her sleep, to prevent it from falling down. She had in her subconscious mind inkling about a possible mishap in case she was not careful enough in her child's safety during such a journey. These thoughts were programmed unconsciously in her brain at the very beginning of her journey. She just followed the action-plan, and behaved that way. It was all instinctive and ituitive behaviour on her part.

Animals are known to behave instinctively. The other day, as was reported, a mother bitch was seen lending her breasts to a needy orphan monkey-baby forsaken by its mother. The innocent baby, probably without recognizing the benevolent donor, was enjoying itself to be part of this philanthropic 'milk donation' scheme where it was the lone beneficiary. The newfound 'mother' was seen enjoying herself even more than the beneficiary. All her typical canine mode of expressions clearly depicted her feeling of pride. It seemed that she had boldly overruled the protests and resentment 'vociferously expressed' by her own pups in order to dissuading her from taking-up this venture. The canine pups, more than the loss of some quantity of milk that is solely meant for them, did not like the idea of sharing their mother's love with an 'intruder'. There might have been sonant exchanges like, "No mummy, no", "No children, no" preceding her final verdict.

In another case, as reported, a monkey and a dog are both members of a human family. The elders in the family go outdoors for work for long hours, leaving an infant son at the care of these two members. Both of them jointly look after the child very well by feeding him with the food that his mother has earmarked for him and kept in the custody of these two. They were his security guards. They seemed to be more devoted to their duties than human guards on employment. The monkey prefers sweet lemon juice to milk. By any chance if the elders forgot to add sugar the monkey would throw it away. We cannot say that it is instinctive behaviour and leave it at that. It is a suspect case of evidence of intuition and reason coming into play. It seems that there is no direct evidence to conclude about the role of intuition as well as reasoning vis-a-vis their actions and reactions.

Plants too exhibit instinctive responses, but human beings may not be able to perceive them. We are, therefore, apt to conclude that they do not have such a capability. It cannot be justified because our conclusions are based on hunch or imperfect imagination. Some plants, we know, exhibit evidence of their having some semblance of instincts. They respond to stimuli. 'Touch-me-not' plants and some varieties of carnivorous plants offer very vivid examples to force us to think that there is something more than their having some sensitive chemicals available with them which do the 'trick'. It might be instincts!

# 8

# Role of Humour in Communication

Manifestation of sense of humour by the human beings in their interacting realms provides one with an inkling of one of their communicative behaviours. It is peculiar and special type of communication. It provides one with an insight into the working of their minds. Its employment is peculiar to humans; other members of the fauna do not possess this faculty. Communication of ideas can be done most effectively if it is done humorously, for humour is as sweet as sugar. Everyone including those who are afflicted by the disease of diabetes likes and enjoys sweetness, even though overdose might induce monotony, sedation or even death to some people, depending upon their levels of acceptance and absorption of sweetness. Similar is the case with humour. A few cases of 'indigestion' due to overdose of it too are reported. Cynics do not enjoy humour; they do not know the art of smiling or laughing, except probably when two cynics share their cynical pursuits. A 'test dose' of humour can be administered to persons to confirm if they are cynics or not. Even though it is a Herculean task to 'convert' such persons, there have been some success stories. The results may not be commensurable with the efforts.

Human beings are endowed with abundant intelligence. It is this intelligence that makes them different as well as superior to all other beings on this earth. Intelligence has its many facets and dimensions when it expresses itself. Whatever we humans conceive, create or construct everyday forms nothing but evidence of its presence in us, though of course, ostensible in different individuals in varying degrees of both quality and quantity. It is, in fact, this element of variance that renders the study of the human minds by humans themselves very challenging and difficult, even though, at times, rewarding and thrilling. Thus, it offers great realms, avenues and opportunities for research scholars. Intelligence manifests itself in human beings in many ways. Sense of humour is one such manifestation. The presence of sense of humour, therefore, provides direct proof of the existence of a good deal of sagacity in persons, while its absence may not mean lack of it. A good joke cracked by an initiator to a target person or group of persons causes a boisterous laughter. But it is not the case always. Sometimes it may produce only a chuckle, a grin or even no reaction at all, despite the fact that the initiator, the target and the humour-content, intensity and other characteristics of the joke are the same. This phenomenon is mainly due to varying perceptibility levels at different times and situations, and mood, primarily, of the target group/lot, and, secondarily, of the initiator and situational peculiarities. An initiator may be any of the following types:

a. Stranger Initiator
b. Familiar Initiator
c. Friend Initiator
d. Comedian Initiator

### *A. Stranger initiator*

Assuming that the humour-content, quality and other characteristics to be constant, we will see that the reaction or response by the target people to joke initiated by any of the four categories of initiators will be of different types and degrees. A 'stranger' initiator, may not excite the minds of people to whom the joke is directed, and bring about humour-sensation in them. The reason for this could be that they are not able to perceive or digest the humour. Most people, while in direct conversation with proper eye-contact, fail to listen to what exactly is being spoken, as at the outset, instead, they spend time mainly only in understanding the 'stranger'. Hence, the resultant response will have to fall short of the desired level. This approach is more noticeable when the persons involved are of opposite sexes.

### *B. Familiar initiator*

A 'familiar' initiator is one who is a less 'stranger'. He obviously had more outings with the target lot on a few occasions earlier. Here the humour-generation response by the target would be much higher than that in the case of the 'stranger' initiator for the same intensity or quality of humour.

### *C. Friend initiator*

A 'friend' initiator is similar to the 'familiar' type, but the understanding between both the parties is very great, thereby humour-generation response is also immense. The target is 'conditioned' by the possibility of reasonably accurately anticipating the intensity of humour-content in a joke which is yet to be sent out by the 'friend'. Here the response is normally positive as well as adequate. The only problem is that there is a chance that the type of initiation and the type of humour could fairly be the same, and that the target might perceive them to be monotonous reiterations. There is an element of mutual inductance or conditioning between the involved parties. This could cause communication barriers. A careful, intelligent and alert initiator will take guard against such anomalous results, in time.

### *D. Comedian initiator*

A 'comedian' initiator is a person who is recognized in the world over as a professional comedian. The mere mention of his name or showing his photograph to the target audience would condition them. For example, if one announces before audience that a famous comedian would be amid them shortly, each member of the audience would start 'salivating'. They would have fully got themselves set to laugh, awaiting the emergence of the comedian on the stage. They even start laughing; sometimes even before realizing as to what the joke is about. There is a 'hypnotizing' effect, so to say. There can be variations and exceptions to this behavioural pattern.

The physical appearance and demeanour of the initiator also have their say in the matter of effectiveness, while administering a joke. If the initiator has a 'not-so-handsome' or nearly ugly countenance, his humour will interest the target group more. It is because of the fact that the humour-provocation initiated by such a person could have been much above the expectation-level of the target group. This is a surprise treatment, a mild shock, all the same, helping the initiator's cause or mission.

In order to avail desired effect, in most cases, a bit of conditioning of the target-minds would be required. The person who initiates a joke or a humorous situation should understand, well before his initiating it, the perceptibility level of the target person/persons. Even a good joke or a humorous situation might get undermined or uncared for, if it is fed to a listener at his imperceptible state of mind. The initiator has to be intelligent as well as alert to make the most of the opportunities or situations in order to attain the effect desired and designed. It is like the 'bowling' in game of cricket. The bowler has to understand the weakness of the batsman facing him to get the latter to the former's trap. The level of satisfaction which the bowler attains when his opposing batsman gets 'back-to-the-pavilion' is almost the same kind as that of the initiator of joke gets when his 'victim', I mean, the target subject demonstrates his pleasant acceptance as well as enjoyment of humour. A boisterous laughter or chuckle thrown out by the subject is the ostensible expression of such feelings. This feedback is his reward. But, unlike in the game of cricket, here both the parties to this 'game' enjoy and cherish, though, probably, the initiator gets the lion's share.

Sense of humour is an asset in the hands of anyone who has to interact with others. It can be profitably employed by a leader or manager to enhance his effectiveness. A manager gets his work done through his subordinates. The work can be got done by two ways, namely, by force, coercion or threat, or by persuasion and participation. Both are probably effective, but the latter enables the manager to deal with human beings as human beings and not as 'two-legged machines'. Let them work and live happily. This is a philosophic approach.

Human beings have affinity for comfort and pleasure. Hence, they have inherent and natural proneness to light-heartedness. A manager must have a keen sense to sense, discern and reckon this light-heartedness. Having done so, he should be able to manipulate these propensities in such a way that he will be able to get them perform adequately. They like to obey a manager willingly who is genial and light-hearted in nature, and who is considered one among them. A manager should become a 'familiar' or 'friendly' initiator, as and when situation arises, but definitely not a 'stranger' or 'comedian' initiator. He is sure to achieve his goals in the most economical, efficient and effective manner.

"A leader is a person who influences a group to follow the course of action he advocates." A leader is always identified with the group of which he forms a part. A person who is the leader of an intellectual group concerned with abstract ideas must be different from the person who leads, say, an athletic club. To get a picture of leaders and leadership, we consider the group situation in which the leader operates. This is not to say that leaders of different groups will have no traits in common or that the person who emerges as the leader of one group is unlikely to become one of any other group. It is, indeed, possible to list some general qualities that often distinguish people who emerge as leaders—they are all active participators in their groups, they are dependable, persistent, self-confident and socially popular. Having these qualities, however, does not ensure leadership in every group, but in many situations, the person who possesses such a combination of traits will probably be prominent contender for the leader's slot. A leader has to be a manager and vice versa. Hence, these two words are synonymatic, and used, as such, in this treatise.

Effective leaders seem to be sensitive and thereby pay enough attention to people, their morale, organizational culture, fostering right kind of values and attitudes in them, providing avenues for development of their competence, and channelling their energies in the right directions. The manager or leader must ascertain for himself if his philosophy and style percolate down the line. He should devise means to know if he is paying adequate attention to 'softer dimensions' or the leadership he provides results in the optimum utilization of human potential and thereby ensuring organizational effectiveness. He should constantly introspect and evaluate his own performance. He is to form-up a second nature in him to look into a mirror often.

Management is what a leader or manager does, and what does he or she do? He or she 'gets things done through others'. That would mean that a leader's main task is getting things done through his subordinates in such a way that he is able to accomplish adequately the responsibilities entrusted to him by his organization. The method and manner in which he does this entirely depend upon him. To aid him in this, he must have adequate professional knowledge and practical experience. Further, he should have mature and pragmatic knowledge of how human minds work, or the least, of how do the minds of his followers work. Thus a leader should become a perpetual student as well as practitioner of practical human psychology. This includes psychology of man as an individual as well as a member of a social group. Management is a 'social process' being carried on in an organization that is viewed as a 'social system'. We are apt not to perceive a person as an individual, instead, a part of a social group, and his being managed is a social process.

All living things are allergic or the least, resentful to any sort of sorrow, pain or discomfort. These form strong stimuli to which they react adversely. These reactions may manifest in different ways, depending upon various other influencing factors. One case of expression may be overt belligerence, while the other, covert dissatisfaction. Others assume their positions on the continuum of these extremes.

Human beings crave to be comfortable at all times, as far as possible this ardent propensity forms an integral part of their psyche-system and it evolves determinants of modes and trends of their behaviour. The man's affinity for comfort, pleasure and happiness is such that any deprivation or even potential threat to its continued enjoyment will render him frustrated. Like in the case of a weighing balance trying to regain its equilibrium after its having been disturbed, the human mind tends to reach back to its previous state, at the earliest opportunity. This effort may be voluntary or deliberate. Men have, thus, inherent and natural proneness to light-heartedness in varying degrees. In some, it may be minimal and underdeveloped, while in some others it may be in abundance and fully developed. All other cases find their places in between these two extremes.

A leader who has to get things done by his people must have a keen sense to sense, discern and reckon his men's inherent and natural proneness to light-heartedness. A bit of introspection, on his part, enables him to empathise and understand as to what goes on in their minds under various stimulating conditions and situations. A leader has to manipulate or manoeuvre these inherent and natural propensities in such a way that he is able to achieve the behavioural pattern from his men according to his designs. Men have to be brought to do work willingly and a good sense of humour at the disposal of the manager makes the led 'hypnotized' so to say, and obeying his commands. These commands will appear to them as pleasant persuasion from their leader, and they are obeyed most willingly.

A leader should become a 'pied piper' with respect to his men. For this, apart from other motivating factors, his sense of humour has a quintessential role to play. He should don a genial air which is nothing but an indirect expression of his pleasant and other positive ways of thinking, as 'countenance reflects the mind'. This may, at times, be wrongly interpreted by his men unless they have full faith and confidence in their leader's intelligence, knowledge and wisdom. Hence the leader, by his demeanour both on and off the working environment, should establish the fact that their leader is really superior to them in most of the fields, if not all. Once this is done, his genial air and demeanour mean all well to them and he will be loved and followed.

A leader should have good sense of humour, both assimilative and disseminative, which he should employ and exploit to the fullest advantage. This is an invaluable resource and asset bestowed with him. He can benefit from it immensely. He is sure to achieve his goals in the most economical, efficient and effective manner. If a manager does not possess this sense and most importantly if he is aware and conscious of this fact, he can inculcate it with full determination and purposive self-training. This, of course, is to be preceded by a change in his attitude and philosophy. It is difficult, but not impossible for an alert, intelligent, versatile person, so is any leader. One should cooperate with oneself in this. That is the minimum requirement.

In order to perform his job as a manager or as a leader, he has to be a good communicator but for which he would fail in achieving his goals. Leading or guiding can be accomplished only by communicating to his followers what his ideas are and what he intends to accomplish. Hence communication is of paramount importance.

# 9

# Indulgence in Counselling

Human beings live in societies; hence social interactions would be necessary. They mutually exchange and share their experiences among themselves. Since the opportunities and experiences vary, some of them gain more information and knowledge about certain situations and hence they become wiser. These wiser ones like to give away in right earnestness their hard-earned wisdom to their fellow-beings with a view to benefiting them. This is a part of social interaction and communication. It is a sign of benevolence and magnanimity on their part.

Counselling is the act of rendering advice, and this is the easiest thing to perform at a 'no-cost' basis. Advice is given to a needy who accepts it if he is convinced of its usefulness. He accepts, enjoys the fruits, and acknowledges his gratitude to the giver of it. He is happy. The giver too is very happy when he comes to know that his advice has really benefited the taker. He feels satisfied in the fact that he could be of some help to the other person. The service rendered in this way is usually considered a 'thankless' one, and it should be so in the eyes of the giver, even though the beneficiary might loudly express his gratitude, if he is benefited by it. If he is not benefited, the advisor will be severely condemned and criticized, even though the giver gave it in earnestness and goodwill, and without any malice. It is good for the advisor to anticipate such repercussions before rendering advice. In fact, he should have carefully selected the right person to receive his advice *ab initio* itself to avoid a boomerang later. In any case, the advice-givers are advised to keep helmets with them to protect their heads, as a precautionary measure to meet any adverse eventuality, should the advice rendered backfires. It could be a dangerous game!

In a society where people live together with a common cause or goal, it becomes duty for each of its members to serve or help mutually. This attitude on the part of each and every member ensures the well-being of the society, thus ensuring its ideal sustenance and existence. Society consists of different types of people with varying levels of knowledge, sagacity and intelligence. There should be equitable distribution of these. Mutual interactions among members of the society ensure sharing this wealth of knowledge. It is obvious that only those who have much knowledge can part with. In this, unlike in other cases, the giver does not lose the portion that he gives out to others. In fact, his capability to give advice will be tested, and thereby his acumen will get sharpened. When the taker gets to know that he is benefited by the advice rendered by the other, he expresses his satisfaction. The gleam on his face depicts the level of satisfaction, by seeing which the giver too gets fully satisfied.

Everybody would be having some specialized knowledge in some specialized field or other. A person with human and humane approach may share and induct these. Some people seek advice from others whether they require it or not. It could be a clever or clandestine move by them to enhance the latter's egoism and thereby create a rapport with them. It is an investment of insurance for any future exigencies. This may produce, sometimes, a recoiling effect. Such people may be thought of as vile or foolish by cleverer or more intelligent on-lookers. This sort of behaviour is discernible in official relationships between officers and their subordinates. The subordinates utilize this frivolous method or pretext of seeking advice for non-existent doubts from their bosses to sublime the latter, obviously to earn their sympathy and subsequently undue favours from them. This also happens in this world!

Solicitation of advice comes about in different manner. Some people may not even know where to 'knock', when they are in real need of some advice, guidance or direction. They remain confused. Some others, on the contrary, dislike availing advice from others, even if they are in dire need of it. Advice is available, but one refuses to take it because of his dogged egoism. His egoism does not permit him to condescend from the high pedestal where he has placed himself on. He thinks it is below his 'dignity', as he equates taking advice to some sort of subjugation, dependency and obligation. This is sheer obstinacy borne out of misconception, misapprehensions and lack of mental development. This is a symptom of some psychological disorder. Such a person is apt to say, "Who is he to give me advice?"

A cynic will not like to share good things, if at all any, with others except, probably, his cynicism. He does not like to give away his expertise and knowledge because they might benefit others. This might cause indigestion to him. He is apt to say, "Why should I advise anybody? I have gained my knowledge by my hard work. If anyone wants it, let him also do hard work and undergo tribulations and thereby earn it. I am not here to make him happy". Similar is the case with selfish people. They are highly suspicious about others. If all members think the way the cynics and selfish do, then the society would remain stale. It will become a congregation of irresponsible members, a garbage heap. One should think that rendering correct advice to the needy is a noble cause. If people lived earlier on this earth too had thought the way these cynics and selfish people do, then humanity would not have taken so many forward strides, the positive effects of which we witness and enjoy today.

There are some people who think that they are highly knowledgeable and sagacious. They have some sort of a superiority-complex. They have a feeling that they can find solutions for any problem that anyone faces. They can not 'sit quiet' without giving advice to someone. It seems that such people have 'itching tongues'. It is their hobby to distribute, so to say, advice to anyone and everyone, irrespective of whether the latter requires it or not. It is unsolicited advice. The main reason for such a behaviour could be that they seek concurrence from others to their feeling of self-superiority, and a stamp of recognition from them to that effect. It is also an attempt to assert their egoism and pride. They seem to underestimating and undermining the level of knowledge and competence which others possess. It is observed that some seniors in some organizations do this mistake of advising their juniors, on personal matters, without the latter's seeking for it. This too is unsolicited advice.

It is not always true that unsolicited advice is rendered just only to project the giver's ego-sense or superiority to the other person. Let us consider the case of two friends. The first 'symptom' of the existence of a good friendship between two individuals is that there will be no ego-clash. Another name for good friendship is compromising. There are certain conditions when unsolicited advice is exchanged between two equally intelligent and sagacious friends. It is, however, always possible that even a high intellectual could forget very important but routine matters. In such cases it is the duty of his good and understanding friend to render him advice or making him aware of the need for initiating some actions in some directions. Whether it is solicited or unsolicited, it is good if he takes his advice and implements it whole-heartedly, not rejecting it outright telling that it is an unsolicited advice. This rejection could be viewed as an unwise, crude and cruel demeanour on the part of that friend. Here it can be seen that more importance is attached to his egoism than to his friendship. He should have sacrificed his egoism at the altar of friendship, if, after a thorough analysis, it is proved the advice is well-intended and worthy of adoption. One thing is clear; there is no place for malice or malfeasance in true friendship.

# 10

# Braggartism

Braggartism is also a kind of communication. Braggartism is boasting, and a braggart is an empty or vain boaster, a braggadocio. It is a skill as well as an art which a braggart has mastery in. Braggarts are good psycho-analysts. They are capable of reading the minds of those around them. They take out an easily saleable variety of brag-stuff from among the many they have in their mental warehouse and serve for consumption and digestion to unsuspecting people. They impress people around them initially till the latter realize the hollowness of the bragging claims. The timing of realization is related to the levels of intelligence and imagination that each one among the 'audience' is bestowed with.

They can successfully shine and survive as braggarts in the company of relatively less intelligent people. They are intelligent enough to scan and measure the levels of intelligence and imagination together with the psychological propensities of those who offer themselves as potential audience. They, it seems, employ some devise for that. Depending on the reading on this measuring meter, they adjust their strategies, tactics and design of their bragging. They accomplish all this spontaneously; they ought to have very alert minds.

Name-dropping is the practice of mentioning names of important personalities or institutions into a conversation, story, song or any other type of communication with the sheer ulterior motive of impressing others. The event being described is usually a lie or a case of exaggeration or distortion. Name-droppers cleverly create a milieu where they could project themselves as the 'real ones'. This strategy is employed to position oneself within a social hierarchy. It is often used to create a sense of superiority by raising one's stature and status. They concentrate on their notional or imaginary accrescence. By implying (or directly asserting) a connection to people of high status, the name dropper hopes to raise his or her own social status to a level closer to that of those whose names he or she has dropped, and thus elevate himself or herself above, or into, present company. Name-dropping can also be used to identify people with a common bond. By indicating the names of people one knows, one makes known his or her social circle, providing an opportunity for others with similar connections to relate. Names can be the ultimate status symbols, and as such, they should be collected and displayed—but one needs to be discreet. Dropped names are like donning false hair or a wig. Badly done, they are obvious and show poor taste. Carefully deployed, however, they work wonders for one's image-building temporarily at least. A big multi-coloured soap bubble, impressive and attractive, will burst and vanish in no time, without any fanfare or ceremony!

While studying at the university, I had a classmate of mine who had shown 'symptoms' of this disease of name-dropping. Those were the days when motor cars themselves were a rare phenomenon. There could not have more than two or three scores of cars owned by that township then. As of now, after half of a century, the number could have swelled to two hundred scores. While we were walking back home after our classes, (and that was our daily routine), on one of such days, he shouted enlisting his ostensible agony and despair, when a luxurious car passed overtaking us, "Look, that is my uncle going in it. I do not know why he did not stop the car and given us lift. Oh, he might not have noticed us." His shouting came out only when he was sure that the car would be at least twenty metres away from us; to a safe distance, 'out of range' or beyond 'striking distance', so to say. At the first instance, I was tempted to give him 'full marks' for this performance of his. After a while, I confronted him a bit cleverly and tactfully with a simple question, "Was that person in that car really your uncle? I know almost all of your relatives. I had never seen him before." He had to confess that he was not his uncle, and that he was trying to impress me by 'pulling a fast one'. He would have been tempted to 'bowl wild bouncers, wides and no-balls' or the ignominious 'bodylines', (to borrow terms from the game of Cricket), at me, if at all he could take me granted for a person having only a limited quantum of active cells in my brain. He did not dare equate my timidity to idiocy, and pass on any of that stuff to me for my consumption. My passive but positive stance would have given him enough inkling of my attitude and approach to life. Nice of him! None studies another just by only one interaction. One has to study holistically by analyzing him from different angles. I did all that to assess his propensities, attitudes and approaches to life in general. As he understood that I had understood him through and through; he stopped dropping names. He proved that he had sagacity too, besides cleverness. Later on, when I had come to know that he had joined a dramatic club, I had wished him great success when he would be a part of the cine world. I had my optimism in this; the optimism borne out of his otherwise excellent performance.

There are cases, for instance, wherein the act of inserting names of any famous persons, cultural organizations or institutions into a conversation in an effort to accelerating the building of rapport with someone, or to make one's self appear to be more important or larger than life. If someone says "Yesterday I met Mr. Gandhi at The Great Tagore Hall Show", he would have been expecting the listener to exclaim, "You attend such shows! Did you really meet Mr. Gandhi? Great!." The statements like, "When I wanted to go to the Lion's Club, my Benz car did not start, I had to go by the other car, Pearl," "If the starter-key of 'Pearl' were misplaced, then I would have had to take my third car; thank God, I was lucky." and so on are meant to mislead the listeners. The listeners are kept on 'hold' to count the number of cars he has had. The statement, "While I was getting down from the train the other day, my book, Golden Treasury, fell right out of my bag and fell on the track" too is designed with similar contents and intentions. Some people get one or two of their teeth capped with gold foil. It is considered to be sign of aristocracy. Such people prefer to pronounce some words like 'teeth', or 'cheat' as 'teeeth' or 'cheeet', stretching their mouths laterally to the maximum tensibility, only to make sure that their so-called 'aristocratic teeth' are shown clearly to the listeners who are made to 'watch' their conversations rather than to 'listen' to them. The reasons are obvious. Some people are habituated to employ their right hands for gesturing while talking about something. They invariably "decorate" fingers on their right hands with beautiful heavy rings. Some ladies use brightly coloured nail polish and do not forget to wear attractive bangles that make 'clang-cling' music notes. To add to the scheme of decorations, they wear expensive wrist watches on their right wrists, instead of the common trend of wearing on the left hand. With all these paraphernalia of decorations, they make hand gestures with these right hands, complementing their vocal exercises, in order just to impress onlookers or listeners. Such persons are more interested in 'showing off' of this sort of vanity rather than concentrate on the subject-matter they deal with in their conversations. These are all expressions of bragging.

The slang usage of words, "windbags" and "gasbags" does denote bragging. By resorting to letting out their 'gas' or 'wind', they are trying to cover-up their inferiority, inadequacies, lacunae, shortcomings, hollowness and vanity. It is nothing but crass hypocrisy. They presume that the listeners are captivated fools, and it is on this presumption that they thrive.

Bragging is considered as an undesirable trait. It is very difficult to get correct information from or about the person who is said to be bragging, because bragging is often a clever concoction or admixture of truths, half-truths, untruths and lies, and hypocritical, hollow, exaggerated, manipulative and vane statements. It is difficult to separate chaff from corn.

Initially at the first interaction, the braggart is not identified as one, even though the listener develops some sort of suspicion, but the person gets benefit of doubt. It is considered a suspect case. It also depends on the level of intelligence and imagination of the listener. On subsequent encounters, the listener confirms the suspicion. Then onwards he will be able to remove the 'chaffs' and get hold of the elements of truth in whatever he states. He has to rack his brain for that. It is passive harassment. The listener increases the percentage of 'discount', and finally he takes the total statements to be expressions of total untruths; a sure case of bragging. In this process, the little bit of truth in the utterances gets into oblivion. He will be discredited. The moment he opens his mouth to speak something, the listener will be tempted to discourage him by telling, for the sake of an 'anticipatory bail', "...and you did that,...and you did not do that" and the like. He is sure to understand that the listener has gauged him correctly. It is total boredom to tolerate a braggadocio. Once a good friend, he will be dumped subsequently in the cold.

In some cases, some genuine self-confident achievers talk truly and genuinely about their unique achievements. They have probably no patience to give time for others to recognize, understand and appreciate their achievements which their listeners are not interested to listen. They harp on them in order to make them listen. Here such people underestimate, correctly or incorrectly, the levels of intelligence and imagination of the listeners. Probably, they are aware and conscious of the fact that this world is full of cynics. They are skeptical about the genuineness of their listeners. They are anxious as well as afraid if their case would be left unrecognized. They dislike taking chances. One might label this sort of behaviour as childishness; but it is certain that they have some minor curable psychological disorders. Such people are unfortunately declared as braggarts.

There is one fact that can not be undermined. Most of the humans are cynical, narrow-minded and self-centred; they have neither time nor willingness to listen to good things about others. They are apt to discount the veracity of what good is being stated about others, and at the same time swell, exaggerate or magnify their deficiencies or drawbacks. If the information emanates from very reliable sources, then the percentage of 'discount' will be diminished, but not to naught. Their manipulative thinking system even converts good points into bad ones. They might say, "You might be correct in the light of your experiences with him; but I do not subscribe to your views. My experiences are different. Anyway, be happy." There is also a morbid tendency to extract sadistic pleasure from unpleasant tidings with respect to others. "Seek, thou shalt get" is the doctrine they like to follow when they search for unpleasant tidings of others. Because of these dangerous traits, they do not see any truth in what others say about others, as their perceptions about others are, as such, myopic. It is convenient for them to rubbish even some truthful statements made by others. In this connection, the following elements may be of importance:

(a) In interpersonal transactions, people seldom pay adequate sincere attention to what others say. They prefer to switch off or disconnect the reception devices of the brain. They often pretend to be listening assiduously, but in fact they try to 'hear' only, and not 'listen'. Their intermittent, "Yes" would give an impression that they are really listening to all that intently. They accord a passive negligence.

(b) Because of the above impediment or handicap, the correct and complete truth in the information will not be registered in the mind.

(c) They fill-up information readily available in their mental warehouse, preserved as precious assets, for completion, cohesion or cognition of this fractured information.

(d) Thereafter, a meaning will be supplied to the whole according to their learning, cognition, attitude and overall perception.

(e) The final output of information will be either distorted half-truths or untruths.

In our society, there is plenty of this tribe of braggadocios. Society is comprised of all types of people. To some extent, these braggarts with their art provide entertainment as well. They are very highly imaginative and intelligent, but their intelligence works often only in a tangential manner. It is interesting to listen to their bragging feats when one does not have anything else to do, but one should have to have a lot of patience to tolerate such people. They are capable of spinning many a yarn.

Bragging is resorted to by both the young and the old alike. Children might brag for many reasons. First of all they might lack self-confidence and bragging makes themselves feel better. By bragging they try projecting indirectly faults on others and uplifting their own spirits; they begin to feel that they actually are something important in this world. It is an effort to know their place in school or at home. By bragging, they will get attention and will feel they belong somewhere. Children could brag about anything ranging from grades to sports and to wealth. If children are lonely, they might be under the wrong assumption that by bragging, people will like them better and they will make more friends. If a child brags he has to be helped gain his self-confidence. He has to be shown that everyone will like him more if he does not brag and he does not need to brag to get attention and feel wanted. Bragging is a disease and it is a vicious one. If a child does not brag, we have to make sure that he does not lose his self-confidence because of other children who do brag. He has to be convinced that he does not need to brag about his achievements in order to be appreciated. Also by praising him at home, he will feel less of a need to brag and will not be affected by children who do brag. Children are very vulnerable and they need love and encouragement. When a child brags, he is sometimes indirectly asking people to notice him and feel proud of him. The parents have to show what he means to them and how proud they really are. Bragging is something that children engage in. This tendency in children should be curbed and nipped in the bud stage lest it should be rendered rampant later when they would be grown-ups. It would also avoid their becoming laughing stock in the society. There would be no use in providing water and manure to a plant that is totally withered and dried-up.

To a great extent, society in which such people live is to blame. Society offers its several special brands of 'behavioural specimens' to its individual members to get themselves compared and contrasted with. As a result, some of them are rendered either diffident or over-confident. The diffident lot will suffer from inferiority complex and the over-confident superiority complex. Both of these traits are formed-up in individuals as perceptual cognitions and as they become conscious of them, some sort of psychological imbalance will be developed. Diffident ones search for something that can serve to compensate; and for this purpose they unconsciously choose the art of bragging out of a few available remedies. The diffident try to 'acquire' while the over-confident try to 'de-acquire'. Those who evaluate themselves as superior become over-confident. They underestimate others and think that they would swallow their vane assertions as they are, without analyzing and ascertaining the truth-content of them. They start believing that they can get away with anything they utter. What a folly, my coutrymen!

There are a few important reasons why some people are prone to bragging. It all depends on their individual approaches to life, evolved while carrying on with the process of living in the world. Some of the factors may be brought out as follows:

(a) Genetic factors.

(b) Socio-psychological factors.

### *(a) Genetic factors*

Genetic factors do influence human psychology and the consequent behavioural output. Individual life is perpetuated by genesis, the scheme of inheritance of various individual characteristics by one generation to the next one through genes. This process carries on perennially. The gene contains characteristic elements of personality of individuals. If the genes with bragging traits are passed on to successive generations, the inheritors also acquire the same characteristic traits.

### *(b) Socio-psychological factors*

Individuals live in society. Society inculcates in its members certain anomalous traits like hypocrisy and selfishness. There occurs a fusion of sociological factors with psychological ones of the individuals. Hypocrisy is the art of concealment of true character or belief. It is acting, feigning to be better than one is, or to be what one is not. A hypocrite is one who practises hypocrisy. It is one of the most commonly observed characteristics of human behaviour, the foundation of which is untruth and falsehood. False sense of pride and prejudices form the rudiments of hypocrisy. Hypocrisy and bragging cohabit harmoniously. Selfishness is another trait that brings about bragging. Selfish people perceive of everything that they possess as big, beautiful, best and the like—they confiscate and earmark all the epithets with positive meanings and ascribe all of them in their superlative forms to their possessions. In doing so, they compromise with many a thing. The ladies brag that their husbands are the most handsome and loving men in the world; the men, their wives are the most beautiful and loving. These assertions are meant for public consumption only. In private situations, they would be busy in searching for epithets with opposite meanings. Similarly, their children are the best in every respect. This is all expressions of hypocrisy in relation to selfishness and in doing so they have to resort to bragging.

I happened to visit the family of one of my closest friends some time ago. It was the day that he had come to know that his only daughter had passed her graduation examination. Hardly had I entered the house, when his wife greeted me very cheerfully and conveyed to me the best item of news. My friend was not present there at that time. "Congratulations! What is the result like?" I enquired. "She has passed with First class with Distinction", was the reply. After a couple of minutes, their daughter came in, and immediately I congratulated her for her passing the examination with Distinction. Her mother standing-by nodded her head cheerfully, absorbing the happiness that I had showered on her child. "Thank you, uncle. I didn't get Distinction, only a Second Division" said the daughter innocently. I helplessly watched the pale face of the mother. I could discern her hypocrisy. The mother is a simple person, but given to a bit of bragging at times.

Braggarts thrive and live on their tongues which are unusually long and elastic and made of muscle tissues that are highly tensible, malleable and invulnerable to fatiguing. The size of their hearts is generally small and because of this they are capable of shifting them at will and ease and planting them anywhere within or even without their bodies according to what particular situations demand.

I happened inadvertently to be in the company of some braggarts. I did not mind being in the company especially of such people when I was looking for some relaxation in my idling times. One can get lots of fun. Anyone can imagine what would have happened. They engaged themselves in their usual business of bragging. They spin yarn after yarn. I sometimes wonder as to how they are able to sustain such behaviour of theirs without exhaustion and monotony. One is free to escape from their clutches or captivity at will when one is convinced that enough is enough. That is a great advantage. I heard one of them vociferously asserting that he never got beaten-up by anyone. One of them present there elected to contradict him, "I saw you the other day getting beaten-up by one Harry when both of you were standing near the Riverside Lodge." Promptly came the clarification that it was true and added that it was the only time such a thing happened. Then another member confronted him by asking as to what had happened on the previous Sunday near the Golden Theatre when a hefty person had kicked you very badly. "Yes, that was only time I could not prevent him from doing so. He was a stupid fellow. But these were the only two occasions where I could not avoid doing anything against." Then another member of the group narrated a third incident similar to the earlier ones. And a fourth one came out with another. He had to agree with all of them. Who can deny accounts narrated by eye-witnesses? He was thus cornered and brought to a situation that provided no escape routes. A pitiable scenario, indeed! I was convinced myself, "Enough is enough" and elected to escape from there. I do not want to imagine what would have happened to me if I had continued to be there with them for some more time. Monotony would have over-taken my intent of entertainment and relaxation.

In the *Encyclopaedia of Braggartism*, there is no mention of the words, 'shame' and 'shamelessness', and because of that braggarts are ignorant of their meanings. Ignorance is bliss and that is why they are shameless with respect to their patented trade. Shame is the 'humiliating feeling of having appeared to disadvantage in one's own eyes, or those of others: fear or scorn of incurring disgrace or dishonour.' Shamelessness is immodesty or ignominy and insensibility to shame. The braggarts do not think of what others think of them when they eloquently express of their unreal exploits. It is like a smart and clever cat closing its eyes while drinking stolen milk. It deliberately thinks, for its convenience, that none is watching and going to catch it red-handed. Intelligent, alert and knowledgeable audience will understand that most of the yarns the braggarts spin have an ending like what happens when someone, curious to find out the size and other features of the 'seed' housed in an onion, trying to peel the different layers of the coverings of it. Onion gives an illusory impression to us that there could be some seed within, because of its beautiful and carefully arranged coverings. The act of peeling ultimately gives one only dismay and provides for the escape of a few drops from his lachrymal glands. An onion does not keep a seed within, and so is the yarn spun by the braggarts! The braggarts think that others are not watching or understanding their performance. Even if they have some inkling that others are aware of their game-plan, they ignore it conveniently because it does not match with their scheme of things; it is inconvenient and 'sinful' for them to take note of such 'anomalies'. They deserve and earn effortlessly the label, 'shameless'.

It seems that they have 'thick skin' covering their entire body and even mind. Let us not be anxious or optimistic that one day the medical research would come up with some magical medicines to melt away the 'extra thickness of their skin' and the consequent weeding out of the entire species from the face of the earth. Others would have to learn to live without these entertainers, if on one fine day the world would be without them! Let us pray to God to render these medical researches futile. Let us have faith in Him, and He will not let us down! Let us 'knock the door, and the door will be opened'.

These braggarts would not have been braggarts, had they ever realized that they are suffering from some disorder or sickness. If aunty had a moustache she would have been an uncle', but aunty can not sport a natural moustache and become an uncle. The braggarts can not change their identity very easily. Bragging is a weakness or a psychological disorder similar to that of drug-addiction, but not as serious as the latter. They can be salvaged by counselling, the main thrust being instilling sense of shame by involving them in situations, real or simulated, where they have to look at life seriously. They have to be brought back to realities of life by cutting them to size; the artificial ill-gotten 'tallness' has to be subjected to 'hedge-cutting'. Even though they contribute to fun and entertainment of people, most of times they prove themselves to be menace, especially when they indulge themselves in anti-social pursuits of cheating innocent unsuspecting people who take their bragging on its face-value. Insurance companies do not have provisions to offer compensations to damages caused by these unscrupulous elements.

All braggarts are hypocrites and all hypocrites are not necessarily braggarts; both of them are undoubtedly shameless. The hypocrites and braggarts manifest their characteristic behaviour not only through their words but in physical demeanour as well. Often both their words and behaviour complement each other. Even some ambitious dumb people are observed to be practitioners of these forms of art; the blind, however, is unable to practise it in the absence of vision. These hypocrites and braggarts try to overdo their performance in order to preventing their 'victims' from having any 'breathing' or thinking time, for, that might upset their game plan. In most cases there might not be any deliberate design on their part to resort either to hypocrisy or bragging; it is a case of force of habit. These hypocrites and braggarts are often not 'natural elements or products'. They are produced by the process of mutation and synthesis, the main agent of which is society. They themselves, probably, more often than not, might be victims of an automatic programming in their minds. They are a helpless lot, suffering from psychological disorder. They are captivated slaves and despite their sincere efforts in terms of introspection, accidental or otherwise, they seldom succeed in retrieving themselves from the clutches of these cursed diseases; even a divine intervention might not help them. Others should have sympathy for them. Let us forgive them. *Sic transit gloria mundane.*

Bragging is the game that hypocrites play. Bragging is the cover they don to keep away their deficiencies, inadequacies, inferiority complexes and the general diffidence from public view. They pretend to be what they are not, and probably they try to express as to what they might be intending to become.

Mohammad Ali said, "It is important that you recognize your progress and take pride in your accomplishments. Share your achievements with others. Brag a little. The recognition and support of those around you is nurturing. It is not bragging if you can back it up." "If you done it, it ain't bragging" said Walt Whitman.

# 11

# Sarcasm, Derision and Insultation

Sarcasm, derision and insultation are members of the same family. They all refer to communication of a profane variety. All of those who practise this sort of undesirable method of contempting others either by behaviour or verbal communication or both suffer from many of the maladies or complexes like selfishness, jealousy, cynicism and egoism.

A sage once set out for a journey through the world in search of 'sin' as well as 'sinners'. After a long lapse of time, he returned to his hermitage, and sat melancholically. Seeing this, one of his faithful and loyal disciples approached him and enquired of him as to why he was in a pensive mood. He said, "My boy, you know that I have been roaming the world looking for sins and sinners, but I could not find a single case or person. After my return, I have not been doing anything worthwhile except a bit of introspection which revealed to me that I have been wasting my time all the while, and at last I could find the only one, here only, and that is I." The disciple was flabbergasted at the statement. He had also observed a sneer on his face. He did not want to provide asylum in his mind to seemingly or likely blasphemous thoughts about his master, even though he was provoked by his master's demeanour. He kept quiet for a while. All electrons got congregated themselves, to manifest their eagerness in helping the inadequately and poorly blinking 'fluorescent lamp' of his brains. Their offer was accepted, and the result was spontaneous brightening of his brain. The disciple understood the depth of what the sage had spoken.

In black and dark background, white objects become whiter and brighter. This world would have been an unworthy and monotonous place to live in, if only good people have been living. Good is good only if bad is beside it. A wise man has once said that one should not move away from the person who is indignant, derisive and contemptuous towards him. If possible, he should build a house for that person opposite to his own; because that is the way he can reform and cleanse himself without soap and water. That person's contempt and criticism will be tantamount to a mirror, wherein he can look and get his drawbacks highlighted and focused. He will thus be able to reform and purify himself. So it is a boon that such persons exist in this world. The black becomes foil for the white.

Sarcasm is a terrible and destructive kind of communication. It usually comes out of a cynical mind. Sarcasm, normally, does not have a truth-base. It emanates basically from one's heart, and not designed by the head. If it is only of the heart, and not from the head, then he can be excused to some extent, for, the latter's role, if any, could be more detrimental. The person resorts to employing this heinous weapon called sarcasm in order to pulling down one in front of others in the society. He gets sadistic pleasure. He manifests his meanness at heart. His satires or jibes speak of the working system in him. This is a disorder. One fine morning, if the head placed on him realizes about his problems, consciously or unconsciously, deliberately or accidentally, then he may tumble upon self-analysis which is the only cure for his disease.

Cynics usually employ sarcasm in whatever they utter in presence of others. The basis of cynicism is jealousy. The cynics do not hide their inner feelings unlike hypocrites. They are jealous of someone else's prosperity which the other person has earned due to his goodness and hard work. What can be done? The minimum that the cynics can do is to envy those who have achieved and by his cynical attitude to derive sadistic pleasure from it. They express their feelings of contempt by overt behaviour. They refuse to recognize other's goodness and do not mind extending this impression to the whole of humanity. Such people do not get proper sleep and are disturbed. Cynics experience bad dreams. Their body-constitution does not provide place for hearts, the space is given on lease to wickedness, malaise and hatred. They are usually surly in their behaviour as well as attitudes. They are prone to looking at people with suspicion. This is also a disorder. They are misanthropes.

Derision is a peculiar behavioural output wherein there is a propensity on the part of some people to laugh at others, thereby trying to gain some ground for enhancing their stature in the eyes of others. Hence this is usually done in public. In fact, they themselves are having the same traits of behaviour as those others whom they laugh at. They use it as a cover for their own hiding. It is smartness or cleverness. In fact, their mocking at others is equivalent to mocking at themselves: they do not seem to understand the same: but others understand the truth. They are resting foolishly in their 'paradise'. Their efforts to make others laughing-stock, recoil on to themselves at times. They are clever, but others are cleverer. They too get sadistic pleasure like cynics and 'sarcasters'.

Derision has two aspects—positive and negative. The positive relates to helping others in subtle way to know what their drawbacks are. Some children, for example, say proudly that they want to become crane-operators when asked about as to what they would want to be when they grow-up. If their parents want them to take-up some other profession which they consider 'loftier', it may be good to laugh at such ideas and deride them repeatedly in light manner when they are in their receptive veins. This sort of derision will bring forth positive results. Deriding people in the presence of others will be tantamount to insultation. This is the negative type. This is the result of superiority complex combined with cynicism on the part of the insulter. Insulters can harvest sadistic pleasure without any sort of labouring and incurring investments.

It is interesting to watch, observe and study the behavioural patterns that these 'sarcasters', cynics, deriders and insulters present to us. All of them have similar traits to manifest. Although they look different, they essentially belong to the same class of people. All of these people are intrinsically of the same material. They developed these behavioural aberrations without their being conscious or knowledgeable. There are many contributory factors, like hereditary and socio-psycho syndromes, bringing about these aberrations. One must have sympathy for them, because they are haplessly mentally sick.

The people who are now deemed 'sarcasters', cynics and deriders might not have been like that, right from the beginning of their lives. They might have subsequently changed to become like these because of their adverse and unhealthy conditions in their family and also social environment. Or they have been mishandled by their 'best' teachers, namely, their haunting and harrying experiences in their lives. They start hating people around, and thereby developing allergy to interacting with them, especially with those who, in their perception, are lucky, successful, progressive, and happy 'neighbours'. Loneliness in old age is another reason for such anomalies.

Even though introspection and self-analysis are the remedies, we cannot easily get around and convince such people to adopt these. They pay no heed to advice rendered by their friends or their seniors, as in the case of any other type of delinquents. Hence counselling by some wise men whom they genuinely respect will have some positive effects. It is a laborious process, because their willingness to co-operate cannot be easily purchased. We cannot afford to discard them; we have to salvage them, because they are problematic to themselves and detrimental to the harmonious existence of society.

# PART III

# 12

# Communication vis-à-vis other Members of the Fauna

Communication in many of its facets is not limited to humans, or even to primates. Every information, i.e. exchange, transmission and reception of signals, between or among living organisms can be considered a form of communication. Animal communication is any behaviour on the part of one animal that has an effect on the current or future behaviour of another animal. Of course, human communication can be subsumed as a highly developed form of animal communication. The study of animal communication has played an important part in the development of ethology, sociobiology, and the study of animal cognition. Although animals communicate, they do not have language like what the humans have. They do make noises but these tend to be situation-related, for example, a loud shriek to signify fear or severe pain. Even humans also have situation-related noises. If an Indian, an Englishman and a Russian, standing blind-folded would make the same noise if anyone stamped on their toes. These are examples of the ways of communication. This is quite evident as humans are able to communicate with animals especially dolphins and other animals employed in circuses; however these animals have to learn a special modified means of communication. Animal communication, and indeed the understanding of the animal world in general, are rapidly growing fields, and even in the current century so far, many prior understandings related to diverse fields such as their emotions, culture and learning, and even sexual conduct, long thought to be well understood, have been revolutionized. Animals can learn human language to some extent as understood recenly with respect to dolphin communication and teaching hand signals to apes. Some dogs are taught by humans to sing songs. It is a pity that the great humans with great level of intelligence are unable to learn the language of the less 'intelligent' animals, instead they have to force them to learn theirs!

Nature tells tigers to hunt, kill, and eat deer; deer to eat grass; elephants to eat vegetation; ants to enjoy sweets; bees to collect honey from flowers and live on it; cows to live on grass and young calf on its mother's milk; birds on fruits; giraffe to stretch its long neck to reach its food, kept above, on tall bushes and trees; plants to draw their food from inside the earth; flowers to look at sun and blossom; micro-organisms to our development as well as destruction, grass to grow on the surface of the earth; rivers to meet water requirements of everybody and everything; and above all, most importantly, Nature to supply air to all under its own is supplied to all under Nature's own personal supervision and control in order to avoid any breakdown in supplies of this vital ingredient. What a flawless organizational set-up our Nature has made!

I happened to observe a cow in a herd. One of them felt an itching sensation behind its left ear. If a human being had the same problem, he would have sorted it out himself or he would have taken help from his willing or unwilling fellow beings. They have some 'audible and understandable' language to come to their rescue. But what of a cow who, as far as we know, has nothing of that sort of a facility at its disposal. But another cow came forward and solved the problem within seconds by a 'tongue action' at the exact point behind the left ear. How did the first cow convey its specific problem to the other and how exactly the other one understood the problem? It is not mere 'instinctive' communication that had taken place? One must better ask them. Probably they 'speak with their eyes'. We often emphatically declare that these animals do not have any intellect and they understand nothing. This is equivalent to a cat's hypocrisy in closing its eyes, while it drinks the stolen milk, pretending that none is observing and going to catch it red-handed. Our bold, but shameless declarations or assertions that animals other than humans do have only instincts unfortunately are one-sided, since no confirmation or otherwise is obtained from the animals. We, for our convenience, take their so-called 'silence' for their non-existent concurrence. Here we are unjust and cruel. This predicament of theirs can be understood only if we have some sense to empathize with them.

Similarly, a female antelope had some vexing problem just below one of its eyes. The male companion promptly solved the problem by employing gently, softly and with care and caution its tough sharp-edged huge heavy paraphernalia called horns. If at all we happen to witness this 'operation', we would have been scared, thinking that these tough heavy sharp-edged horns could cause damage to the eyes of that female. We would have only wonder to fill our eyes and hearts; nothing untoward happened! It is a fantastic experience to watch such a phenomenon.

When wildest of wild animals like lions and tigers stealthily move about looking for their prey, the monkeys 'supervising' and 'circumspecting' all happenings from tree-tops make loud noises and move and jump from branch to branch or tree to tree, giving alarm to the hapless potential preys about impending danger, so as to enable them to run to safety. Even birds join monkeys in the latter's pursuit for this 'noble cause'. All these mean communication.

It is interesting to watch hundreds of birds fly together in beautiful perfect formations, like our fighter planes do. There are a few cases wherein fighter planes in such air displays had met with accidents by collisions, whereas in the case of the birds, there have been no such cases. The latter unlike the former has modern devices of communication with the help of which they do a lot of manoeuvring in the air space. These birds maintain the same speed as well as distances between and among them while flying. They definitely have some communication system though incomprehensible to humans. It is, in any case, fascinating spectacle!

Birds communicate with one another in a series of ways. Vocal communication by means of calls and songs is the most important way. Generally, all birds have a voice and they use it to call or sing. Birds use their calls mainly as signals to other birds. Baby birds call in one way to tell their parents that they are hungry, and another way to convey if they are hurt or frightened. A male robin sings a song; it will mean for another male a call for fighting to defend its territory; a female listening to the same will get ready for mating. They all may sound alike to humans. Even in a crowded colony a parent bird can single-out the voice of its chicks and the chicks can recognize that of their parent. Some birds mimic other sounds in the surroundings. Certain birds like parrots and mynas become mimics when in captivity. They can even be trained to imitate human speech and whistling. Some birds communicate by sounds other than vocal sounds. They resort to visual displays like flashing of tail feathers used in courtship. A peacock spreads its beautiful feathers into a gorgeous fan and dances during courtship to attract and invite peahens.

'Other' animals too have emotions like humans. We can often notice the eyes of goats that are given a notional extension of life-span by few minutes, by the butcher, while another one is being butchered in front of their eyes. They do not seem to cry. They also do not laugh, but their eyes occasionally gleam, a semblance of a smile, when they are happy. Lambs frisk and play, when they do not face dangers. It is, probably, not due to any mental deliberations, but it occurs instinctively and instantly. We are not sure if there is any element of mental work involved in it.

Communication is the cause and behaviour is the effect. Communication is the stimulus and the behaviour is its corresponding response. One is the action while the other is the reaction. If one watches a behaviour, one can reckon the communication process behind such behaviour, an indirect way of understanding. Moreover, it is true of animal communication. The behaviour seems to depend on patterns of reaction with which they are born, called instincts and reflexes, there being no role for intelligence to play. After breaking out of its cocoon, a moth flies about and finds its food in the juices of plants without having to learn how to do so. Instinct directs the animal to do certain things to stay alive. Intelligent animals like apes, monkeys and dolphins learn to solve their problems with the help of their intelligence, besides the power of instincts. In this, they rely on previous experiences. Animals use their senses to receive communication from others of their kind and interptret them. Some other animals use their scent in the same fashion. Members of canine and feline families define and proclaim their territorial sovereignty by urinating on the boundaries. Some animals use their face and body to communicate. An angry gorilla may throw leaves into the air and beats its chest with its fists. Elephants communicate with one another in various ways of posturing and gesturing. They make different kinds of rumbling sounds; a hoarse loud one when they are frightened, a low humming one to calm young ones. Many mammals, in particular, have glands that generate distinctive and long-lasting smells, and have corresponding behaviours that leave these smells in places where they have been. Often the scented substance is introduced into urine; sometimes through sweat. Cats have scent glands on their flanks, and deposit scent by rubbing their sides against objects; they also have scent glands on their foreheads. Other instances include the warning cries of many monkeys, and the mating calls of many species of frogs. Baleen whale sounds may be the loudest produced by any animal and may travel for tens or hundreds of kilometres underwater. These sounds may be for long-range contact, assembly calls, advertisement for mates, greeting, location and availability of food, threat, or individual identification.

System of communication prevailing in the community of ants is very intriguing. Ants that live inside plants or in the leaf-nests may tap their gasters against the outside walls of their nest when they discover food or enemies. Such taps arouse the insiders who rush-out of the nest within seconds to carry food inside or fight the enemy. They may even produce squeaky or buzzing sound to complement the taping sound. Ants also communicate with one another by giving out a sensitive chemical called pheromones with different kinds of smell and taste, each kind communicating different information like food availability or presence of enemies. Often one can see ants conferencing and sharing information. Within seconds of the death of another living being including humans, a particuar type of ants assemble at the spot for a sumptuous meal. One wonders at this spontaneous congregation. This behaviour of theirs gives ample proof of their unbelievable communicating capability. In the case of death of a human being, it is they who declare the person dead even before a doctor could do so. Hundreds of them assemble near the dead body abruptly to make and share a dinner or supper uninvitedly. Ants can tell a colony-mate from enemies by odour. When two ants meet they smell each other with their antennae. If they are nest-mates they stand mouth-to-mouth and exchange pleasantries. It is interesting to watch tiny ants with very 'hot news' about availability of their favourite 'item', sweets, somewhere in the vicinity, doing to-and-fro brisk walks between two points to convey the news to their kith and kin. Within seconds all of them reach the rendezvous to share the happiness.

A bee discovering a plentiful supply of nectar several fields away from the hive returns and gives directions to its fellows by flying in the direction of the source in a series of complex patterns in front of the hive. The other bees will then fly straight to the food source. Bees carry with them a pouch of material from the hive which they release as they re-enter, the smell of which serves as 'gate pass' for their safe entry into the home-hive. It is communication that has the final say.

The most spectacular thing about blue whales, probably, is the big sounds they make. Scientists have measured the low-frequency sounds they make when they communicate with each other by using a decibel meter. Some of their vocalizations have been recorded as loud as 188 decibels and can be heard as far as 850 km away. To get an idea of just how loud 188 decibels is, we can compare it with that of the sound of 120 decibels that a commercial jet makes at the time of taking off. Human shouting is 70 decibels; sounds over 120 decibels are painful to human ears. That makes whales, by far, the loudest living thing anywhere on earth! Blue whales emit very loud, highly structured, repetitive low-frequency sounds that can travel for many kilometres underwater. They are probably the loudest animals alive, louder than a jet engine. These songs are meant to communicate to attract mates and may also be used for informing other whales of availability of large masses of krill that they eat.

## Functions of Animal Communication

While there are as many kinds of communications as those of social behaviour, a number of functions have been studied in particular detail. They include:

- Everything to do with contests and aggression between individuals.
- Many species have distinctive threat displays that are made during competition over food, mates or territory; much of the bird-songs function in this way. Often there is a matched submission display, which the threatened individual will make if it is acknowledging the social dominance of the threatener; this has the effect of terminating the aggressive episode and allowing the dominant animal unrestricted access to the resource in dispute. Some species also have affiliative displays which are made to indicate that a dominant animal accepts the presence of another.
- Courtship rituals are signals made by members of one sex to attract or maintain the attention of potential mate, or to cement a pair-bond. This demeanour frequently involves the display of body parts, body postures, or the emission of scents or calls, that are unique to the species, thus allowing the individuals to avoid mating with members of another species which would be infertile. Animals that form lasting pair bonds often have symmetrical displays that they make to each other.

- Many animals make "food calls" that attract a mate, or offspring, or members of a social group generally to a food source. When parents are feeding their offsprings, the latter often display begging responses.
- Alarm signals made in the presence of a threat from a predator, allowing all members of a social group, and often members of other species too, to run for cover.
- Metacommunications are signals that modify the meaning of subsequent signals. The best known example is the 'play face' in dogs, which signals that a subsequent aggressive signal is part of a play fight rather than a serious aggressive episode.

### Interpretation of Animal Communication

It is important to note that whilst many gestures and actions have common, stereotypical meanings, researchers regularly seem to find that animal communication is often more complex and subtle than previously believed, and that the same gesture may have multiple distinct meanings depending on context and other behaviours. So generalizations such as "X means Y" are often, but not always accurate. For example, even a simple wagging of domestic dog may be used in subtly different ways to convey many meanings such as:

> Excitement, Anticipation, Playfulness, Contentment or enjoyment, Relaxation or anxiety, Questioning another animal or a human as to intentions, Tentative role assessment on meeting another animal, Reassurance ("I'm hoping to be friendly, are you?"), Brief acknowledgement ("I hear you", or "I'm aware and responsive if you want my attention"), Statement of interest ("I want that food, toy or activity, if you're willing"), Uncertainty or apprehension, and Submissive placation (if worried by a more dominant animal).

Combined with other body language, in a specific context, many gestures such as yawns, direction of vision, and so on all convey meaning. Thus statements that a particular action "means" something should always be interpreted to mean "often means" something. As with human beings, who may smile or hug or stand a particular way for multiple reasons, many animals reuse gestures too.

### Intraspecies vs Interspecies Communication

A sender and a receiver of a communication may be of the same species or of different species. The majority of animal communication is intraspecific (between two or more individuals of the same species). However, there are some important instances of interspecific communication. Also, the possibility of interspecies communication, and the form it takes, is an important test of some theoretical models of animal communication.

### Behaviour vis-à-vis Communication (Fauna)

Any behaviour indicates communication and any communication results in behaviour. Animal communication is any behaviour on the part of one animal that has an effect on the current or future behaviour of another animal. The study of animal communication, sometimes called 'zoosemiotics' (distinguishable from 'anthroposemiotics', the study of human communication) has played an important part in the development of ethology, sociobiology, and the study of animal cognition. The best known forms of communication involve the display of distinctive body parts, or distinctive bodily movements; often these occur in combination. So a distinctive movement acts to reveal or emphasise a distinctive body part. A parent bird bringing food, for example, and presenting its bill and tapping on the ground in front of the nest elicit begging response from its hungry chicks. It is the result of a learning process on the part of the chicks via rewards. Another important form of communication is bird-song usually performed mainly by males which is the best known case of vocal communication. Other instances include the warning cries of many monkeys, and the mating calls of many species of frogs.

### Prey-to-Predator Communication

It is interesting to watch some of the systems of communication between prey animals and their predators. A wasp uses its bright colours together with attending gestures to warn its predator that it can cause harm to it. The predator chooses to keep away from it, succumbing to the threat potential in the warning. Its previous unpleasant experience too might become a deterrent. It is more interesting to watch hoverflies coloured in the same fashion as that of the wasps, but without having their stinging faculty, mimic the wasps and get away. Some of the members of the canine species adopt aggressive postures, such as growling with their teeth bared and successfully get better of their predators. Rattlesnakes rattle to warn potential predators of their poisonous bite. A few animals like chameleons change their skin colours smartly within seconds to match those of the surroudings and thus avoiding detection in order to hoodwink their enemies. Sometimes a behavioural change and warning colouration will be combined, as in certain species of amphibians which have brightly coloured bellies and capabilities of adjusting the colour of the rest of the body with that of the surroudings. When confronted with a potential threat, they show their belly, indicating that they are poisonous and they mean 'business'.

Another example of prey-to-predator communication, is referred to as a pursuit-deterrent signal. Pursuit-deterrent signals occur when a prey indicates to a predator that pursuit would be unprofitable because the signaller is prepared to escape; "Here-do-I-go, catch-me-if-you-can" attitude. Such signals can be an advertisement of its ability to escape. Pursuit-deterrent signals provide a benefit to both the signaller and receiver; they might be able to prevent the receiver from investing in a costly pursuit that is unlikely to result in capture; they without wasting time and energy might be able to prevent the sender from clever fleeing. Pursuit-deterrent signals have been reported for a wide variety of fish, lizards, rabbits, rodents and birds.

Some predators communicate to prey in ways that change their behaviour and make them easier to catch, in effect deceiving them. A well-known example is the angler fish, which has a fleshy growth protruding from its forehead and dangling in front of its jaws; smaller fish try to take the lure, and in so doing are perfectly placed for the angler fish to eat them.

# 13

# Communication vis-à-vis Members of the Flora

I had sprinkled some chilli seeds in an earthen flower pot kept in the balcony of my flat. Some of the seeds germinated and tiny little plants came up, and as they grew up they started flowering. The balcony is a closed one with sliding glass shutters. I had kept one of the shutters open, to allow a bit of sunlight and fresh air to come in. They had practically no direct contact with the mother earth, but for the gravitational force. I was worried as to how pollination would take place, as the pot was not in the open, which fact would have prevented the flowers from 'inviting' the pollinating agents. To my surprise, pollination took place. But, despite my keen watching, I could not see any pollinating agent arriving and doing the 'work'. I could get what I wanted—fresh green chillies from my 'mini garden'. Who called the pollinating agent to come there and do its 'job'? The invitation of the flowers to the pollinating agents to enjoy their hospitality is, again, a case of communication: with the favourable response from the pollinating agents a two-way communication is complete. None should wonder if there is some communication between flowers of a plant and the pollinating agents by means of some unknown media. The scent they send-out, the colour they exhibit and the sweetness of nectar tasted earlier by themselves or the experience of taste relayed, recommended and communicated to them by their benefactor-friends could be the media. Whatever may they be, the receivers get the messages right, and they are motivated to perform the required 'duty' entrusted to them by Nature—pollination. It is the great Nature that has brought about this phenomenon. One would suspect if Nature has developed some sort of invisible website or resorted to some kind of clandestine communication! One would often get excited by thinking about the various games that Nature plays.

Plants too engage themselves in communicating. A 'touch-me-not' plant, for example, responds the moment anyone touches it, by folding all of its leaves spontaneously, to scare away its 'enemy'. We have known about how carnivorous plants behave. Communication is observed within the plant organism, i.e between and among plant cells, also without between plants of the same or related species, and between plants and non-plant organisms, especially in the rootzone. Plant roots communicate in parallel with bacteria, with fungi and with insects in the soil. On a more basic level, there is cell signalling, cellular communication, and chemical communication between primitive organisms like bacteria, and within the plant and fungal kingdoms. All of these communication processes are sign-mediated interactions with a great variety of distinct co-ordinations. Fungi communicate to coordinate and organize their own growth and development. Additionally, fungi communicate with same and related species as well as with nonfungal organisms in a great variety of symbiotic interactions, especially with bacteria, plants and insects.

# PART IV

# 14

# A Speaking Bed

"Many people have incorrect inkling that I am synonymous with laziness or inactivity. But, I, in fact, form one of the most important ingredients of happy and healthy living. When I get dressed-up, I often look pretty, cozy and luxurious. By looking at me, one's imagination catches up, and goes in my favour, gets him attracted to me and enjoys sharing life with me. I am one of the few things in anyone's life which provide him with comfort. Though everyone is vulnerable to this force of attraction, the effect on different people are of variant magnitudes. The weak and the aged worship me as their primary god. A lazy man, whose primary end in life is to 'conserve' energy, both mental as well as physical, becomes my best friend. A dormant child is normally very happy to be lying on me, though the child symbolizes activity and life. My friends and I occupy an important place in hospitals. There the patients even prefer us to doctors. When people are tired, sleepy or sick they look eagerly at me. Nobody or nothing other than I can solve their problem of getting rid of discomfort or pain. There is no substitute for me. While enjoying the comforts provided by me, they feel indebted, definitely at least up to the time they leave me behind. Their gratitude may be transient. They are reluctant to extol or even praise the valuable and timely help rendered by me. The beneficiaries are ungrateful. They should praise: if not, at least, desist from denouncing or despising me.

Most of the females of the fauna conceive their offspring in their wombs. Initially they are in the embryonic stage, and some time later they become foetuses. When the foetus develops into a miniature baby, the mother delivers it out. Some of them lay eggs that are intelligently kept in some secure places, away from their enemies. Various members of the fauna resort to various systems and methods, some are very unique and peculiar, in ensuring safety of the eggs. The crocodiles and the sea-turtles, for example, have habit of laying their eggs in pits that they make on the sandy seashore. Before they go back into the sea, they carefully and cleverly cover those pits with sand, to provide a camouflage effect in order to hoodwinking their potential enemies. It is often the case that these clever enemies succeed in unearthing the eggs and making good meals of them. Nature allows a percentage of these eggs to be consumed by them. The mothers too are aware of such happenings. They console themselves in a philosophical way that they too do the same thing with other creatures. The loss is thus compensated. Similarly, tiny sparrows make very cute looking nets, hanging precariously from twigs and branches of trees that hang-out into air-space of rivers and lakes, wherein they ensure safety of their eggs. After the lapse of pre-determined duration of time, the offsprings emerge into the world, after breaking the outer protective walls of their lovely delicate fortress called the shells. It all happens like certain chemical chain reactions occurring between and among some chemicals, taking place under certain conditions of temperature and pressure. The chain reaction takes place automatically similar to those due to human indulgence in bringing about pyrotechnics. It is all very interesting and intriguing!

But, in case of flora, offsprings are conceived and procreated generally in their flowers. Each tree or plant has many flowers, the number ranging from unity to several hundreds, and each flower has eggs securely placed in its ovary. One can say that each flower represents a procreative unit, and each tree can be considered as a cluster, a family or even a mini society. The eggs situated in the flowers are to be fertilized by union of male counterparts. In case of the fauna, the males and females move about and facilitate such unions.

But, unfortunately, members of the flora are forbidden by their Creator from moving around. "You don't move around and waste your time. All of your requirements like food, water, oxygen, carbon di-oxide will be met at the spot wherever you are asked to stand. For the purpose of procreation and perpetuation of your species, I shall make foolproof arrangements. I will be sending some mini-creatures who will be entrusted with the job of collection and distribution of necessary pollens to all of you. You see, I have supplied to each one of you with very sweet-smelling and tasting 'mundane' nectar called honey. These mini-creatures are nonchalant care-free loafers who can easily be satisfied if you allow them to get themselves fed by some honey which they love to consume. You are to be grateful to them for this great help they do for you, but you should not expect any gratitude from them in reciprocation. They are not aware as to what an important and specialized job they are performing. They are fools living in their paradise. They think that they are great looters who, in broad day-light, loot your this precious possession of honey. They invite their friends and relatives too to join them in these looting enterprises. They take you for innocent and foolish ones, because you do not show any feeling of eagerness, despair or frustration. Poor things! Let me confide in you, it is all done this way only for your benefits. I like to perpetuate this system", the Great Creator confides this fact in the members of flora.

These mini-creatures include butterflies, bees, beetles, insects, squirrels, sparrows, and many others. They all derive pleasure and satisfaction by entering the inner-most chamber of the flower, and steal the honey kept there. They used to talk among themselves about how 'foolish' these flowers have been in keeping open the entry door of the chamber where they keep such precious things as honey. They should have known that there are shrewd ones, like themselves, awaiting to make most of such golden opportunities. Their satisfaction is similar to that of a panther that stealthily hunts, kills and eats its innocent, unsuspectful and helpless prey. These flowers have the last laugh. And who is fooling whom? Nature distributes duties to various agents, depending upon various factors of criteria like the size of the flower, quantum of honey available in each flower to match the requirements of the visiting agents, the size of the beak or tongue, weight and other physical characteristics of the agent vis-a-vis those of the flower. A tiny agent, for example, is allotted to a tiny flower. As the tasty and sweet honey is kept quite deep in the flower, these beneficiaries have to work hard to reach there and earn it. There will be numerous pollen grains present *en route* their glorious and enticing path leading to the location where the honey is stored. In this process, the tiny pollens stick to their feet. The honey they get in the first flower will be just enough to serve only as appetizer. Hence they are forced to move to another flower. When they reach the second flower, the accompanying pollens get dropped there. The 'job' as required by the flower is thus 'done'. This process continues. Nature's game-plan is successfully accomplished.

Even wind, rain and wild animals also become agents, performing such philanthropic acts inadvertently, while they move about purposelessly amidst them in the jungle. They are out there on their errands. They do not care for the honey these flowers keep. All the same, they too join this pollination campaign unconsciously. Happiness! Indeed, it is all immensely interesting and intriguing observing and understanding!

After the pollination process, the flowers get 'pregnant' and offsprings are born in the form of seeds, equivalent to eggs of the fauna. These seeds are kept hidden within sweet fleshy coverings called fruits. These fruits have very attractive colours that can invite anyone towards them. Even their very looks speak loudly that the invitees would have sumptuous feast. These are advertisements which serve to entice some prospective customers. Cigarette manufacturers ape the techniques of marketing that these flowers follow. They offer free cigarettes to non-smokers and get them converted to smokers gradually. Once anyone of these invitees tastes one of these sweet fruits he is sure to get addicted like the non-smokers turning smokers. They even spread the news about availability of such a thing, and encourage others to accompany them to the fruits. All sorts of 'salivating' aspirants from the fauna world are helplessly attracted towards them. It is indeed interesting to note that none from the flora world is interested in these fruits, probably because they are not allowed to move about at will to have any access to them, unlike members of the fauna. They might enjoy their juice if someone can manage to make it accessible to their sub-soiling roots, for, it is on these roots they have their 'mouths'. They would be happy to recycle its contents, after disintegrating various elements present therein by chemical processes. It is the rain water that takes the juice to the place where these chemical processes take place; the place where the roots are.

The smaller invitees like mosquitoes, flies, ants, birds, squirrels sit on these fruits and eat, while the bigger ones like monkeys, big birds like vultures and wanton boys pluck them, and eat and enjoy the feast to their heart's content. Management of industrial units, in human context, allows their employees to make dwelling units nearby the industrial units, keeping the objectives of mutual benefit. Likewise, the tree leases out space and the needed infrastructural and structural support to those benefactors who choose to become residents on it. The host provides them with even building materials such as dry twigs and leaves as a good gesture of help in making their temporary homes. It is all good picnics for them. The mother tree enjoys the music and orchestrations that these guests create. It will be like a colonial set-up that human beings form up. In many cases of human colonies, the host organizations have been brought to grief and repentance. The population in these colonies gradually increases, and with it many discords, disputes, quarrels and squabbles are bound to be generated among themselves. The initial musical entertainment turns itself into disturbing noise pollution. The host tree understands the situation very well, but never resents or repents for this self-inflicted malady. It seeks refuge by adopting a philosophic approach, and recognizes its inevitableness. General observers might consider all this as hypocrisy on the part of the host tree. One can only request them for empathy.

Most of these invitees do not like the seeds kept within these fruits, and hence they discard them somewhere randomly and carelessly. They move from one fruit to another, and to another and so on, till they feel that they are fully fed and satisfied. Despite the fact that even a single fruit can feed one fully, each of them likes to feed on many to enjoy variety and avoid monotony. When things are available in plenty, anyone would be confused as to where to start from and where to end at. It is like a child who is sent into a room full of several attractive toys, getting confused as to which one to be taken into possession. He would like to have all of them at the same time. He picks one and then finding another more attractive, throws the first one and takes the second. This process of acceptance and rejection continues. This is what happens when things are available in plenty, very much in excess of requirements. This is what these guests feel and do. This can result in strife and confusion. The mother tree coolly and keenly observes all what is happening. It wanted all these things to happen that way only.

The seeds discarded by these beneficiaries are thus scattered all over the ground. They germinate at the appropriate time. They await the monsoons to set-in when they get their water requirements. Thus new plants or trees are born, and when they grow up, the same system or cycles are followed. In some cases, the offsprings are born from stems or roots of the mother trees. All of them resemble their mothers in all respects. In both these cases the mothers continue to live till old age takes their lives away, or till they are brutally murdered by unscrupulous, wanton and selfish humans. All these new plants grow up near the place where their mother lives. The mother and her children thus form a society there; the society gradually turning into a jungle or forest.

Unlike my older sisters, I am born from the womb of my mother. I am a caesarean-born child of my mother. My mother's case was not an exception to the general statement by surgeons, "The operation was successful, but the patient died". I was survived by my mother; I am the unfortunate daughter of a pre-deceased mother! My older sisters used to condemn and curse me telling that I was responsible for mother's death, a stigma I have to live with.

My sisters do not know who their father was. Even I do not know who my father was. In any case, it is sure that all of us are not born of the same father. I do not even know if someone has to father a child. The nurses on duty in the labour-room where I was laboured have told me that my mother was slim, elegant, gracious and good-looking. In her youth, she would have competed in beauty pageantry and won laurels. I grew-up as a beautiful young lady. Even when I was only a child, I remember, several beauticians used to visit our place to beautify me. They used to get me clad elegantly, and appreciate my beauty, like the way humans appreciate their young beautiful daughters in their bridal attire. Humans take their daughters to some famous beauty parlour to enhance their beautiful looks, as part of scheme for their 'value addition' which is a prelude to the visit of prospective bridegrooms. In my case, there used to be regular visits of such prospective grooms. I used to get fed up with such exercises. I was accepted finally by a famous hotelier. He took me with him to his hotel. It was beyond my imagination to conceive as to what would await me there in the hotel. I had prepared myself to face whatever was in store for me, good or bad.

On reaching my new home, they call it starred hotel, I was taken to a room on the ground floor of this five-storied building and asked to wait there for some time. It seemed that they were trying to find the most suitable room for me. After a brief waiting I was accommodated in the second level of the hotel mansion. The room was air-conditioned as you can expect. I knew there would be someone to share the room. A few minutes later, there came my partner. We were told to lay ourselves together adjacent to each other. Both of us liked the idea. Both of us were of the same age and looked like twin-sisters. She too was born in the similar manner as I was. Thank God, I had someone with whom I could interact freely and share my thoughts. My partner too might have thought in the same manner. After some interactions with each other, we came to know that we had the same philosophic approach to life, and that we were made-for-each other.

After a few months, I was transferred to one of the very elegant rooms in the fifth level. I was disappointed because I was afraid to lose the company of my friend. I had requested the management to allow my old partner to be my roommate. They had good sense to grant me my request. Till she was given marching order to share my room, I was restless. I was very happy to see her along side me. We were asked to be very close to each other, as we were in the old room. This proximity enabled both of us to live together, once again, in the same old way.

I want to share with you one of the incidents that I have had witnessed there. This relates to some highly confidential matters, and, therefore, I will share with you only if you promise me that you will not divulge these to anyone. These are the stories that pertain to human beings, and I choose to keep the names of people involved too strictly confidential. Human beings, you see, are prone to taking revenge on anybody and anything without any rhyme or reason. They are intelligent but wicked and vile. Their Creator has created them so. I do not know why, nor am I interested in knowing about it all that.

Sharing secrets is always a thrilling experience for anyone. When one is convinced that he is elevated as a confidant of someone, especially someone who is the 'Ultimate', one would experience the greatest of bliss. Females are found to be more inclined to share secrets with other females. Some of the so-called 'secrets' may not have any real content of secrecy. It is probably the manner in which the matter is introduced and narrated that makes it look like secrets. All the same, they take a solemn promise from the other person, the hapless victim, before such sharing of secrets, to the effect that the latter would not divulge them to any one under any circumstances. In all such cases, the latter spontaneously agrees and undertakes such an agreement, even showing ostentatious willingness to sign on dotted lines, due to immense inquisitiveness of knowing what the secrets would be. Both of the parties involved in the agreement, in fact, are fully aware that these promises are meant to be broken. The sayer definitely wants it to be broken. It is hypocrisy. It used to be a common occurrence in primary section of schools where one small girl accosting another, taking her aside to a corner, and pouring into her ear some relevant or irrelevant story, giggling without any sense, making gestures conveying deliberately to some other friend standing slightly away that they were sharing some secrets, most likely about that person, and making that person embarrassed. What she might have told her in her ear might have merely been, "The earth is round".

On behalf of my tribe, I can say that all of us feel proud of ourselves whenever we find that we are of some use to some needy persons. We really enjoy ourselves while offering our services. But we feel unhappy when we see that our services are utilized for fructifying some sinister designs by our occupants. At mid-night some of them indulge themselves in calumnious conversations about most others existing outside their bedroom. We beds are forced to eavesdrop some of these 'pillow-talks' that take place. Lying on the bed, some vile wives or female friends exploit their romantically surcharged partners, and get them agree to fulfil some of their evil, unjust, illogical, menacing and selfish desires, taking full advantage of the latter's 'weak moments'. We welcome anyone who comes to us seeking help. We consider ourselves magnanimous and guest-keen.

In one of the evenings, a young man accompanied by a young lady came in to occupy us. I do not know if they were a married couple. I was not concerned about it. Both of them had started drinking some alcoholic liquid. They had emptied their glasses many times. They were engaging themselves in some arguments on some matters which I did not understand. The gentleman was struggling hard to stand up and talk like someone of a preacher. He had managed to stand erect to fall back on me helplessly. It seemed to me that he was trying to practise some physical exercises. He was quite a bit intoxicated. The lady was complaining about a person who was following and harassing her. He, young man, suddenly got infuriated and told her that he would eliminate him. The lady agreed. Both of them decided to hatch some designs to get rid of him.

After some time, they were interrupted by the sound of the door bell. They responded by opening the door. It was another young man. From the welcoming demeanour of both, it was clear that he was an unwelcome intruder. They did not like to be disturbed by this intrusion. Suddenly the young lady conveyed by gestures to his friend that he was the same person she was talking about. The friend suddenly pounced on the stranger, and they engaged themselves in fist-to-fist fight. The lady hit the intruder on his head with a rod that she could get hold of. The man fell unconscious and died on the spot. It was a horrifying scene. Leaving the dead body there both of them vacated the room and went away. Next morning, some police men were brought in by the manager of the hotel. We were the only eyewitnesses to the incident. The police asked me to provide an account of what had happened; and I did. I do not know what happened to that case.

There are many more incidents of this nature, but I do not want to share information on them with all of you, for, they would look like monotonous re-iterations. I continued to serve the hotel till the hotelier felt that we became too old to serve there anymore. He then sold both my friend and I to a businessman whose was dealing in old ones like us. He too took the services of some beauticians to make us look beautiful. We had felt bad for having been sent out from the hotel, but we were helpless. Our stay there in the businessman's was very short. After a month, we were sold out to a house-holder. I was happy because I did not have to leave my friend behind. We used to discuss as to what would be our life like in the new environment. There we knew that we would have to serve only one master. We were told to be part of the children's room. We felt very happy at this decision of theirs, because both of us always loved children. There were two good and naughty children, a boy aged seven and a girl four, in that house. The girl had a habit of wetting our linen every night. We did not mind that because there was no foul smell emitting. When their parents go away on work, these children used to jump and play on us. They were very happy children. We could share their happiness. We had enough rest when these children would go to their school between ten in the morning and four in the evening. During this period we had enough time for interactions. We exchanged pleasantries as usual. The lady used to clad us in beautifully designed clothes every morning. We used to look neat and tidy always. It was a good life.

Our guests include ants, cockroaches, bugs or any other organisms. In this case too, we feel unhappy when we see that all these miniature guests convert our broad chests to battlefields where they organize blood-sucking campaigns on other occupants. Some of the samples of blood they had collected prior to the start of the campaign were tested to confirm 'positive' for alcohol contents. Such blood is seen preferred by them.

Most of the things that humans possess, including the most intimate ones, escape their notice, despite the fact that they are unconsciously aware of their presence in and around them. Once they are removed from their original place by someone else they become alert, and notice their absence. The presence is not noticed, but their absence is. This is the case with me too. They daily depend on me. When they require me, they look for me. If I am not available then they come to know of my importance. They get awareness in the absence of a thing, and not when it is readily available. They become nostalgic about the thing, when they miss it.

It is on me, Somnus, the Greek goddess or Nidradevi, the Hindu goddess rests and sleeps. It is very essential for human beings for their conjugal consummation which is the basic need for their procreation. While one is lying on me one's body and mind really relax and refresh, giving a soothing effect, which will encourage and stimulate cool thinking and the resultant good decisions. It is on me many kings and emperors used to take important decisions. Once one is on his bed in his bedroom he is left alone to himself without any external influencing factors. He is at peace.

Most of the humans believe that we are merely a carpentry creation and are inanimate objects. We are much more than that. We have sentiments of affinity, empathy, sympathy and love for all. We are very caring. We beds can be anything to lie or sleep on, and it includes mattress, a bedstead, a couch or even a garden plot. You might have heard of phrases like 'bed of roses', 'bed of thorns' that are figuratively used by imaginative people. Don't you know when a valiant soldier who sacrificed his life at the altar of the honour of his beloved motherland is brought from battle-field and is laid to rest in 'bed of honour'? We feel proud of such moments. We too get chances to honour such great souls. We feel honoured to be part of such august moments."

Thus an inanimate object, like bed, is personified and thereby enabling it to narrate its saga of existence, in an autobiographical mode.

> The bed is a bundle of paradoxes: we go to it with reluctance, yet we quit it with regret; we make up our minds every night to leave it early, but we make up our bodies every morning to keep it late.
>
> —Charles Caleb Colton

# 15

# A Canine Perspective

"From time immemorial, we dogs have been the best friend of the human beings. Millennia ago all members of the fauna were wild. The human beings used to live in caves or improvised huts in jungles. In fact, the earth used to be covered with either forests or naked deserts. Rivers used to flow through the forests. For the very existence of both flora and fauna, they needed water, besides air. Hence forests came-up near water resources and the fauna settled down where both water and forests were available. That is why all human civilizations had flourished all alongside the courses of rivers. None of members of the fauna could settle down in the deserts, for obvious reasons. All of them had the same kind of living style. They lived mainly on fruits and roots of plants; and some of them on their hunt-proceeds.

Most of the wild among wild members of the fauna used to hunt and kill other animals and ate their meat for their livelihood. Initially, the homo-sapiens used to be hesitant hunters. Gradually they too took to hunting small animals. They ate raw meat probably in the absence of fruits and roots. There used to be forest fires which killed many animals, besides mass destruction of the flora. It was, probably, accidentally that they happened to taste meat of some animals that were roasted alive by such forest fires; and so also when they found that there were no plants to provide fruits and roots or living animal-preys seen anywhere in their neighbourhood for hunting. It was the survival instinct that made them to eat this roasted meat. They found it very tasty. That marked the end of their eating raw meat. We dogs belonged to the canine clan. We were physically weak as compared to other animals in the jungle. Our only weapon we had, besides our canine teeth, was our capability for loud barking which we employed in scaring our enemies. But our enemies knew, as you too, "Barking dogs seldom bite" that was what our plight was. The tigers were very fond of our flesh, and, therefore, they never allowed us to live in peace. All know that cats and dogs always maintain belligerent stance with each other. In fact, this truth can be extended to the entire feline and canine species.

We found that humans, though small in size and weak in bodily strength, as compared to many other animals like the elephants and horses in the forest, by their high level of intelligence, were able to conquer and make all of them their slaves. The greatest surprise we experienced was when we saw the huge and the mighty elephants were tamed and trained by those humans and made them their most obedient slaves. It was a great sight when they used to discipline these mighty elephants with the help of a stick of nearly a metre in length. Mounting on them, the humans used to take them to the forest and utilized their services while they went hunting. Unbelievable!

Understanding all this, we decided to depend upon the humans. For this we had to prove that we meant no harm to them. We had to struggle hard to convince the humans in this regard. It might have taken many centuries for that. Initially, after mustering courage, we had started sleeping outside their caves, once they went inside to retire. Throughout nights we used to be awake, as though we were guarding them. Many a time, we had raised alarms to those humans sleeping inside their caves about the presence in the neighbourhood of a tiger or some other enemy. They had thought initially that we were a nuisance and were chased away by them. But we were not discouraged. After some time they had realized that we had meant all good. It was nothing but a mutual benefit scheme. We were terribly afraid of such ferocious creatures, and we knew for certain that the humans would chase them away. This sort of things had happened many times. The humans thus recognized our sense of sincerity and loyalty, and understood that we had the quality to become their security advisors. They also understood that we would one day become their loyal servants. We used to eat their 'left-overs', proving that we never had any intention to interfere and snatch their food. We had proved to them that we were at their mercy only.

It all took many years before we could muster and win their confidence. We did all this at the cost of losing our hunting skills. We slowly developed a dependency syndrome vis-a-vis the humans. There was not even an iota of sense of sacrifice in whatever we did at that time, only a *quid pro quo* arrangement under a *sine qua non* situation. The human beings, in this respect at least, were not hypocritical, and they called a spade always a spade. That was how we dogs earned a permanent place in their hearts and with that we had cast off our initial cautiousness, skepticism and hypocrisy and became genuine beings. We would never vacate that place in their hearts, nor would we be allowed to do so by them. Our bondage of friendship is millennia old, and it has stood the test of time.

These humans asked us to help them in hunting. They used to take three or four of us with them into the forest. It used to be quite a thrilling experience. They made use of our sniffing capabilities to their good advantage in locating their hiding preys. We used to walk a few metres ahead of them, leading them, giving an impression that we were the actual hunters and they were only our followers. We all used to spend the whole day hunting, and in the evening we all used to return with our fortunes in the form of those unfortunate victims. We all then shared the hunt-proceeds happily. The life went on like this. We had our own language and we used to discuss all hunting strategies among ourselves. The humans could get an inkling of what we wanted to convey to them. We could not talk the language they spoke, but slowly we developed some sense to understand what they wanted to convey to us. We became experts in understanding their body language and gestures, and they started understanding ours too. It was all a happy situation through and through. We had developed identical understandings on most of the issues.

Both of us started enjoying our companionship and comradeship to a very great extent. Millennia rolled off, and friendship too carried on. The human nature underwent a lot of changes. Their concept about their dwelling places too changed drastically. They gradually developed first-hand scientific knowledge on the changing climatic seasons and day-to-day weather conditions. They started cutting trees of the forest, making the land naked and barren. The vastness of the forest contracted and shrunk, and the wild animals kept retreating, keeping pace with the backward movement of the forest. The humans started constructing their houses with solid materials. Then onwards they did not have to be afraid of the attacks from those wild animals. There used to be sporadic incidences of attack by the wild animals, mainly to give expression to their displeasure and anger due to what the humans had done to them. If any one of a human, venturing to undertake an independent analysis, would come to realize that he has caused irreparable damage to Nature due to his thoughtless acts. He atones for all these now, though belatedly.

The humans cultivate friendships also with some other animals like cats, cows, buffalos, horses, elephants. The cats belong to feline clan, other members of this being *felis leo* (the lion) and *felis tigris* (the tiger). The cats are *felis domestica.* They are highly ferocious and they normally do not like to contract long standing friendship with anyone including the humans. They can, probably, be tamed to be good companions only if they are adopted in their younger age. We are not like that. The humans know this fact very well. The human beings attach a bit of philosophy when they claim that they foster these other animals just because they are also created by God, and that they love them for love's sake only. Here we suspect a bit of hypocrisy on their part. They love them, but their love is not unattached. They seem to be attached to the benefits they reap from those relationships. The cats help the humans in eradicating menacing rats and rodents, the cows and buffalos give them milk, the horses give them entertaining sports and travels and the elephants help them in doing hard labour. These animals are docile and good-natured, and they all thus serve the humans in various ways. We have no competition with them in any area. Our clan is a very special type, and none can be compared with us. That is why the humans have given us a very special status. We are greatly grateful to them for it.

People say that our name often stands as synonym for high degree of loyalty, friendship and trust-worthiness. All have respect for us. We are not cunning like cats, *felis domestica,* and with which we have occasional fights. The cats tease and deride us. We are physically stronger than cats, but in our fights we don't win as they cunningly climb nearby trees and escape defeat. We cannot climb trees. We are simple and innocent in nature, unlike jackals, foxes or wolves of our own canine family.

Human beings keep home-pets most common of which are dogs, cats and rabbits. We dogs become the obvious first choice. They keep us in pairs. We often request them to keep both the sexes of the same breed in that pair, enabling us to have some sort of romance and married life. It is our right. Don't you agree with us? Mostly they oblige us. Some of them do not have any sense, and to their liking, they keep a male Alsatian with a female Pomeranian thus depriving us of a possible alliance. We have our strict ethical and moral codes prohibiting us from such relationships. It seems that keeping home-pets serves as status or fashion symbol among urban affluent human families. The urban human females are very fond of us. It is generally observed that the madams take us out for walk through the streets of the city, probably because it is a way to 'show off' their vanity. They provide us with very rich food. It seems they bathe us in warm water, applying some special variety of soaps. The manufacture of these 'special' soaps is the monopoly of some particular type of firms who carry out aggressive marketing strategies by advertisements, addressed mainly to these madams. They claim a lot of advantages in using the particular soap. These madams fall in their traps; and purchase such soaps; they do it without consulting us. We have no problems. We enjoy the bath; needless to mention about their soft touches and the humming of some light music. They get us clad in expensive and beautiful outfits. Even the belts fastened around our necks are well-decorated and attractive. These innocent and thoughtless lots do not understand that we do not enjoy these things. OK, we ignore these!

They love us and treat us as members of their family. The 'man' and his 'woman' in the house become our foster father and mother. In fact we become their children and they our parents. It is needless to say we too love them. Whenever visitors come, we will be formally introduced to them, "Look, Goldie and you, Mildie, meet your uncle and aunty. This is your uncle, and this is your aunty. Come, shake hands with them." After obeying the instructions, we wag our tails and sit near them for a while, till we get marching orders, "OK, now you can go away to your room and play." Thus we get opportunities to practise what they had taught us earlier. We could hear their appreciative words about us and our behaviour, "They are very cute and lovely. You have trained them well. It is fantastic", they offer their appreciative comments. Our 'parents' feel elevated and satisfied. Some people feel jealous of our lifestyles. They consider us to be very lucky, and they would have wished themselves if they could also get a life like that of ours. Even some humans too cursed their bad luck in not having been born as dogs like us. In any case, other members of our canine family would definitely have been very envious of us. When Goldie fell sick, our 'parents' sat near her throughout the night, nursing and attending on her. A veterinary doctor was summoned; and got her treated. But unfortunately she died. I felt very sad, but more than that, our 'parents' could not bear the loss. They did not eat any food during the entire mourning period of three days. They had withdrawn themselves from all entertainment activities in or out of the house. They wept in front of her photograph that they had taken only a few days before her death. Some visitors came to the house to condole the death of their loved one as well as to console their friends at these trying and grieving moments.

Most of us are chained whenever we are taken out for a walk, usually by our young 'mother', and the ends of such chains are held in her left hands while walking. She is afraid that we would run away from her. Why should we run away when we are cared so much by her? Where else can we get such royal treatments? She is unimaginative and short-sighted. Poor lady! She keeps on talking to us in some incoherent language, which we sometimes take for soliloquy. She gives commands to us, loudly, "Goldie, no, no, get away; come this way." We obey those commands to oblige them. These madams, nay, 'mothers' are happier in the company of those of us who are huge and ferocious-looking or tiny and cute. There is a hidden agenda in this. They too can get a lot of attention from the human male onlookers. A handsome onlooker might enquire as to what the age, height, weight, breed and so on about us, knowing fully well that these topics would please the young lady. He might not be interested in the answers to the questions; at best, it would be an excuse to 'gate-crash' into her heart. They make us look down upon those of our less fortunate and destitute members of our clan, moving around aimlessly on the streets. They are unable to hide their contempt for them.

Most of us have the good or bad luck to share their beds. Young ladies in the house get into arguments among themselves as to who out of us should share their beds. We can understand if unmarried girls fight among themselves in this matter; but to our surprise, young married ladies too get into competitive spirit. It is blasphemous to think that they prefer our company to that of their husbands. Anyway, it is more than pleasure to be sleeping with them. They caress and kiss us. Our saliva left behind at places where we lick can cause infections. Knowing this, we hesitate to kiss or lick. Their expression of love sometimes gives impression that they are trying to compensate or supplement the love they receive elsewhere. It is wrong to suspect that it is case of sublimation.

Childless parents normally like to adopt a human child from some orphanage. This is done probably to fill in the existing vacancy of a child in the family. Or is it because they are very fond of children, or is it because that they want a successor to inherit their large assets, or throne as in case of kings, once when they would cease to exist? Whatever may be the reason best known to them, they adopt children. It is the lady who has to take a final decision about 'whats and whens' of adoption. Some of them may not like to adopt a human child at all, as some of these barren ladies go cynical and decide to adopt one or two of us instead of human babies. They do not mind declaring that they prefer puppies to human babies because they perceive that the former will be more affectionate and grateful. We are lost to understand as to why they expect or demand gratefulness from the adopted. Only those who do favours should expect the favoured to be grateful. None of the adopted would have requested anyone that he should be adopted as a favour. Adoption is done to satisfy the adopters' own interests. This fact should be clearly understood by them well before the adoption. There is no *quid pro quo* arrangement in this. This is no commercial transaction. Humans are requested to pardon us if we have transgressed our limits while expressing our views in this manner. We know that human beings are magnanimous and sportive, and they like frank criticisms and opinions irrespective of sources they come from.

It may be very interesting to know that some crazy human beings arrange our marriages like they do in their cases. In India, marriages are solemnized with a lot of fanfares and celebrations. Our marriages too are celebrated that way. It is said that some erstwhile rulers of some small states had been doing it. It seemed that they had nothing else worthwhile to do. They used to announce the dates and venues of such marriages and it was made compulsory for their subjects to attend them. They used to beautify the 'bride' and the 'bridegroom', selected from among us and clad them in beautiful robes; they were made to wear wedding garlands in the traditional way. They even arrange our 'honey-moonings' too. It was an occasion for them to rejoice. These people foolishly imagine that we too enjoy all this. In fact we feel harassed while undergoing such ordeals. What can be done to make them understand our precarious predicament?

The humans are very fond of mountaineering. They take some of us with them while they go for such pursuits. We too enjoy such outings. In this way both of us get good companionship. This is an opportunity for us to strengthen our bondage. We welcome always any such enterprises. We get opportunities to eat some new fruits, and so also to see some new species of flora and fauna. What a thrilling experience!

We are asked to perform some specialized job as well. These humans train us to detect criminals perpetrating undesirable activities in the human societies. Here, they make use of our greatest faculty, sniffing. Seeing us at site of the crime, the behaviour of the criminals around will be one of bewilderment. The degree of bewilderment on the face of each person gives an indication to his or her involvement in the crime. This is the psychological side of it. When we help them in catching the culprits; they feel happy and proud of us. They feel grateful to us. We feel satisfied as we think that we were of some use to our masters. In some cases, we are given awards for our meritorious services, while we serve police forces. The awards are normally given to human beings. We are given enhanced pecuniary allowances as well in such cases. Here the satisfaction of the giver only is considered, and not of the receiver.

The humans use acrimonious language to their fellow beings when they get angry with them. They start abusing each other. We pity them when they take our family name in the midst of abusive words. They call each other "dog" as an abusive word. O, Lord they don't know what they are saying and hence please forgive them. During such altercations one tells the other that he would kill him and cut him into pieces and throw them to feed dogs. What an acrimony it is! We wonder how they can use this word, 'dog' as an abuse, especially when they know quite well that we are one of the best creatures in the whole of fauna-world. The humans ascribe names of some amidst them whom they hate, dislike or contempt, like "Hitler", or "Stalin". They feel happy when we answer them when they call us as such; probably they could never have dared uttering those names when those people were alive.

They, however, forget their ill-feelings about such people thanks to our gentle affectionate responsive behaviour. We, on the other hand, feel proud to be named after such 'fantastic' historically important people. It is very little that we can do to prevent them from misusing our names this way. We can only feel sad and pitiful.

We are the ultimate and most popular pets, because of our very enthusiastic, attentive, loyal, loving, friendly, playful and amusing nature. We have earned this elevated status by our sincerity and hard work. No other pets should envy us. We ask for little but return many times more than what we get. We expect the bare minimum from our owner or family. They should be prepared to give us the care and commitment we need.

Rashmi, the little daughter in my new 'family' has adopted and brought a new five month-old guest-puppy. They gave her a human name, Lina. She automatically became part of the household, and all members started treating her as such, and involve themselves equally with her. No separate status was given to her. Two of us were already members of the family.

**Some Funny Incidents**

We don't know if this is really that funny, it probably happens to a lot of others too. One day we saw Lina keep staring at herself in the mirror! It was a tall mirror, set up against the wall and there's a space behind it, and she kept staring at herself and barked and scratched and thought another dog was there! The cute part was that she went behind the mirror to check if the dog was actually there! Though we also had similar things when we were also young puppies, we laughed and laughed.

Once on another occasion, she hid an ice cube in her blanket and was very upset that it was gone a little while later.

She kept moving and dragging the blanket looking for the ice cube. She did not know that ice would melt and vanish. Poor girl!

While at the vet, Dr. Vetman was holding Lina and talking to her about what a well behaved little girl she was. He was supporting her bottom in his hand. As he gave her a treat, she peed in his hand. Silly girl!

The hospice was established by the Monk Bernard of Menthon in Switzerland near Alpine pass, a few centuries ago in the service of travellers getting trapped in heavy snowfall or avalanche. The monks who maintained it, discovered that the St. Bernards, that was the name given to them then, were good companions to have with them during the night searches and during storms. They had learnt to find the paths with unerring accuracy. They had great agility among the rocks and boulders of this mountain region, and could carry loads of supplies for the monks and the hospice. And they possessed such an acute sense of smell that they could locate victims of avalanches three to six metres under snow. They made huge contributions to mountain rescue work, by augmenting the work done by the monks. Afterall, they are some of us. We salute the memory of the great St. Bernards!"